MW01707204

2004 SUPPLEMENT

CASES AND COMMENTS

CRIMINAL PROCEDURE

SIXTH EDITION

by

JAMES B. HADDAD
Late Professor of Law,
Northwestern University

ELIZABETH P. MARSH
Professor of Law
Quinnipiac College of Law

JAMES B. ZAGEL
Judge, United States District Court for the
Northern District of Illinois

LINDA R. MEYER
Professor of Law
Quinnipiac College of Law

GARY L. STARKMAN
Attorney-at-Law, Chicago, Illinois;
Former Assistant United States Attorney,
Northern District of Illinois

WILLIAM J. BAUER
Judge, United States Court of Appeals
for the Seventh Circuit

FOUNDATION PRESS
NEW YORK, NEW YORK
2004

THOMSON
WEST

395 Hudson Street
New York, NY 10014
Phone Toll Free 1–877–888–1330
Fax (212) 367–6799
fdpress.com
Printed in the United States of America

ISBN 1–58778–774–1

TEXT IS PRINTED ON 10% POST
CONSUMER RECYCLED PAPER

TABLE OF CONTENTS

TABLE OF CASES

Principal cases are in bold type. Non-principal cases are in roman type. References are to Pages.

*

2004 SUPPLEMENT

CASES AND COMMENTS

CRIMINAL PROCEDURE

*

CHAPTER 2

CONFESSIONS AND INTERROGATIONS

A. VOLUNTARINESS OF CONFESSIONS

Page 48 Add new note:

Consider the en banc decision in United States v. LeBrum, 363 F.3d 715 (8th Cir. 2004)

■ HANSEN, CIRCUIT JUDGE

After thirty-three minutes of questioning, Michael LeBrun confessed to naval investigators that in 1968, while he was enlisted in the United States Navy, he strangled to death his superior officer, Ensign Andrew Muns, on board the U.S.S. Cacapon after Ensign Muns caught LeBrun robbing the safe in the ship's disbursing office. . . .

Muns and LeBrun served as shipmates during the Vietnam War aboard the U.S.S. Cacapon. Ensign Muns served as the disbursing officer, and LeBrun served as the disbursing clerk. On January 16 or 17, 1968, while the U.S.S. Cacapon was moored in the Subic Bay, Muns disappeared. After conducting an investigation into Muns' disappearance, the Navy concluded that Muns had stolen $8600 from the disbursing office and had deserted. Thirty years later, still unconvinced of her brother's wrong-doing, Muns' sister convinced Special Agent Peter Hughes of the Naval Criminal Investigative Service ("NCIS") Cold Case Homicide Unit to reopen the investigation.

In the fall of 1999, NCIS agents conducted four interviews with LeBrun. On each of these four occasions, LeBrun cooperated with the investigators and voluntarily answered questions regarding Muns' disappearance. On three of these occasions, he was given his *Miranda* warnings by the interviewers. During an interview conducted on November 20, 1999, LeBrun told NCIS agents that he realized that he may have been involved in the death and disappearance of Ensign Muns. LeBrun also told the agents that he felt that he had repressed memories, and he asked Agent Hughes if he knew of a therapist who could help LeBrun recover those memories. After completing the first round of interviews, the NCIS agents did not have any further significant contact with LeBrun for approximately ten months as they continued to investigate other leads. By September of 2000, however, the NCIS had focused on LeBrun as the lead suspect in the case. At that time, NCIS agents decided to interview LeBrun again.

On September 21, 2000, NCIS Special Agent Early and Corporal Hunter of the Missouri Highway Patrol arrived unexpectedly at LeBrun's place of employment. Hunter told LeBrun that he and Early were conducting an investigation and requested that LeBrun accompany them to the Missouri Highway Patrol office to participate in an interview. Although the officers did not tell LeBrun the subject of their investigation, LeBrun agreed to accompany the officers because he thought that the officers might be investigating certain criminal allegations concerning LeBrun's employer. At the officers' suggestion, LeBrun rode in the front seat of an unmarked patrol car to the station house. The door was unlocked during the trip, and LeBrun was not restrained in any manner.

After they arrived at the patrol office, but before they went inside, Agent Early told LeBrun that he was not under arrest, that he was free to terminate the impending interview at any time, and that he was free to leave at any time. He was also told that he was subject to audio and visual recording anywhere inside the building. The officers then took LeBrun inside the office to a windowless interview room. The authorities had prepared the room prior to LeBrun's arrival, adorning the interview room walls with enlarged photographs of scenes from LeBrun's life. After LeBrun took a seat, NCIS Agents Early and Grebas identified themselves and initiated the interview. At no point immediately prior to or during the September 21, 2000, interview did the agents recite to LeBrun the *Miranda* warnings. The district court found that the decision not to warn was a conscious one made by the interviewers. Special Agent Early testified that no warning was thought necessary because it was not an under arrest custodial situation.

Despite the agents' failure to recite the *Miranda* warnings, LeBrun testified at the suppression hearing that at the time of the interview he understood what his *Miranda* rights were. LeBrun also testified that at the time the interview commenced he believed that he was not in custody and that he was free to leave at any time. The government concedes that the officers used psychological ploys during the course of the interview to facilitate a confession. For example, the agents told LeBrun that he was the prime suspect in Muns' death and that they had significant evidence establishing that LeBrun was the killer. The agents also told LeBrun that a protracted trial in a distant district would drain his financial resources and would ruin his family's reputation. At no point, however, did the agents shout at LeBrun or use physical force against him. After approximately thirty-three minutes of questioning, LeBrun confessed to the crime. LeBrun explained that while he was robbing the safe, Ensign Muns walked into the disbursing office. He confessed that he rushed Muns and killed him by strangling him and then smashing his head against the deck of the disbursing office. At the agents' urging, LeBrun then physically reenacted the robbery and attack. He also explained how he had dumped Muns' body and the missing money into a tank of caustic fuel oil to dispose of the evidence.

After LeBrun confessed to the killing, Agents Early and Grebas asked whether he wanted to apologize to Muns' sister, Mary Lou Taylor, who had flown in from Milwaukee to assist in the interrogation if it became necessary. He indicated that he did. Dr. Taylor, accompanied by Agent Billington, who was posing as Muns' brother and whom the agents had told LeBrun was stricken with cancer, then entered the interview room. LeBrun acknowledged to Taylor and Billington that he was responsible for Muns' death, and he apologized. After the agents had completed their questioning, LeBrun consented to having his house searched. LeBrun then withdrew a cellular telephone from his pocket and called his spouse. The agents drove LeBrun to his house and searched it. After conducting their search, the officers left LeBrun at home. They did not arrest him that day.

LeBrun was arrested at a later date and charged with felony murder in violation of 18 U.S.C. § 1111. . . .

* * *

The facts surrounding the confession are straightforward. LeBrun confessed to strangling Ensign Muns after only thirty-three minutes of questioning. Neither Agent Grebas nor Agent Early was armed during the interview. The agents never shouted at LeBrun or physically threatened him. The government concedes that it used psychological pressure to facilitate a confession. The district court correctly recognized that the type of psychological pressure Agents Grebas and Early exerted on LeBrun here did not alone render his confession involuntary. *See Astello,* 241 F.3d at 967–68 (holding that tactics such as subjecting a suspect to psychological pressure, making false promises, playing on a suspect's emotions, and using his family against him did not render a confession involuntary). The district court concluded, however, that these tactics, when coupled with certain statements that Agents Early and Grebas made concerning nonprosecution, rendered LeBrun's confession involuntary. The critical exchange occurred as follows:

LEBRUN: So, am I hearing that I won't be prosecuted?

GREBAS: That's what you are hearing.

LEBRUN: Is that what I am hearing?

GREBAS: That's what you are hearing.

EARLY: If it's [the killing of Ensign Muns] spontaneous and that's the truth, you will not be prosecuted.

GREBAS: That's absolutely right.

LEBRUN: I am here to tell you there was no premeditation.

EARLY: All right.

LEBRUN: It was spontaneous.

EARLY: Okay.

GREBAS: So it was, let me get this clear. It was spontaneous?

LEBRUN: Correct.

GREBAS: If this is true, then you killed him and it was over, it was over the money; is that right?

LEBRUN: I don't know what it was over.

(R. at 65–66.) The district court noted that the agents qualified their representations by stating to LeBrun that it was only "possible" that LeBrun would not be prosecuted. The district court explicitly did not "make any findings as to what-if any-promise was actually made, or what the legal effect of any promise [was]." (R. at 83–84.) Instead, the district court found only that "LeBrun *believed* he would not be prosecuted if he confessed to a 'spontaneous' murder." (R. at 83.)

Applying the facts as found by the district court to the controlling legal standard, we conclude that LeBrun's confession was not compelled because a defendant's mistaken *belief* that he could not be prosecuted does not render a confession involuntary. *See United States v. Kilgore,* 58 F.3d 350, 353 (8th Cir.1995) (stating that defendant's mistaken belief that he had been promised leniency would not render confession involuntary); *Winfrey v. Wyrick,* 836 F.2d 406, 411–12 (8th Cir.1987) (concluding that defendant's murder confession was voluntary even though defendant was encouraged to talk because of erroneous *belief* that if the shooting was accidental it would negate an element of the offense), *cert. denied,* 488 U.S. 833, 109 S.Ct. 91, 102 L.Ed.2d 67 (1988).

Even assuming that a reasonable person would view the Agents' statements as a promise, a promise made by law enforcement "does not render a confession involuntary per se." *Simmons,* 235 F.3d at 1133; *see also Tippitt v. Lockhart,* 859 F.2d 595, 598 (8th Cir.1988) (concluding that defendant's confession was voluntary despite officers' promise), *cert. denied,* 490 U.S. 1100, 109 S.Ct. 2452, 104 L.Ed.2d 1007 (1989). A promise is merely one factor in the totality of the circumstances. *See Simmons,* 235 F.3d at 1133 (stating that a promise made by law enforcement is only one relevant consideration). Whatever the facts of an individual case, our polestar always must be to determine whether or not the authorities overbore the defendant's will and critically impaired his capacity for self-determination. Thus, it is not enough to show that the authorities' representations were the but-for cause of a confession. *See Schneckloth v. Bustamonte,* 412 U.S. 218, 224, 93 S.Ct. 2041, 36

L.Ed.2d 854 (1973) (concluding that a but-for type analysis is inadequate because "[u]nder such a test, virtually no statement would be voluntary because very few people give incriminating statements in the absence of official action of some kind"). Therefore, even assuming that the agents' statements could be construed as a promise and that the statements induced LeBrun's confession, our inquiry remains the same: whether the facts surrounding this interview demonstrate that the authorities overbore LeBrun's will and capacity for self-determination. This is a very demanding standard, and we are of the view that the facts of this case do not rise to that level.

We have previously concluded that a promise not to seek execution or a promise not to prosecute failed to render the confessions of similarly situated defendants involuntary. For example, in *Tippitt,* we held that the government's promise to a defendant not to prosecute him for capital murder in exchange for a confession did not render the confession involuntary in light of other facts showing that the interrogation was brief and that the defendant possessed an eleventh grade education. *See* 859 F.2d at 598. We do not think it unreasonable to assume that the psychological pressure exerted on the defendant in *Tippitt* to render a confession and thereby avoid execution would be at least as great as the psychological forces presented in this case. In *United States v. Larry,* 126 F.3d 1077 (8th Cir.1997), we held that the defendant's statement implicating himself as being a felon in possession of ammunition was voluntary even though it was induced by a promise that the defendant would not be prosecuted for a separate offense involving a drive-by shooting. *See* 126 F.3d at 1079. The facts of this case are no more compelling than those in *Tippitt* or *Larry.*

We place substantial weight on the fact that LeBrun confessed after a mere thirty-three minutes. Thus, this is not a situation where the officers wore down a defendant's will with persistent questioning over a considerable length of time. We also place significant weight on the fact that LeBrun testified that he had a subjective understanding of his *Miranda* rights at the time of the interview. *See Simmons,* 235 F.3d at 1133–34 (stating that a particularly compelling fact militating in favor of finding a voluntary confession was that defendant understood his rights). We also place substantial weight on the fact that LeBrun was a sophisticated individual with legal training. LeBrun was fifty years old at the time of the interview. He has served in the military, attended five years of college and one year of law school, and worked as a manager in a real estate office. As we have noted, "one of the key concerns in judging whether confessions were involuntary, or the product of coercion, [is] the intelligence, mental state, or any other factors possessed by the defendant that might make him particularly suggestible, and susceptible to having his will overborne." *Wilson,* 260 F.3d at 952. Generally, we have concluded that where the defendant possessed at least average intelligence, then his inculpatory statements were not compelled. *See, e.g., United States v. Gallardo–Marquez,* 253 F.3d 1121, 1123–24 (8th Cir.) (concluding confession was voluntary where defendant was of average intelligence and had prior contact with law enforcement), *cert. denied,* 534 U.S. 1031, 122 S.Ct. 570, 151 L.Ed.2d 443 (2001); *Astello,* 241 F.3d at 968 (concluding that confession of an eighteen-year-old was voluntary where he had completed eleventh grade and possessed a capacity to understand what was being said during the interview); *Simmons,* 235 F.3d at 1134 (concluding that confession was voluntary where defendant had full scale I.Q. of 88); *cf. Wilson,* 260 F.3d at 949 n. 4 & 952–53 (finding involuntary confession where defendant was mentally retarded, his overall mental abilities were in the bottom two percent of the population, and testimony revealed that he could be "talked into anything").

In addition to possessing average intelligence, LeBrun did not display any unique sensitivity that would indicate that the agents might overbear his will. LeBrun had met with NCIS investigators on four prior occasions. The videotape of the interview demonstrates that LeBrun was composed and aware of his surroundings and the circumstances confronting him. In fact, as LeBrun and the Agents discussed the potential statute of limitations problems, LeBrun became more animated and much more interested in the interview. After watching the videotape, it is apparent that LeBrun is an intelligent, calculating person who erroneously perceived a potential loophole in the prosecution's case and tried to take advantage of it by confessing to "spontaneous" murder. Whatever his motivation, it is clear to us that LeBrun's capacity for self-determination was not impaired. Thus, the district court erred in concluding that LeBrun's confession was involuntary.

* * *

■ MORRIS SHEPPARD ARNOLD, CIRCUIT JUDGE, with whom MCMILLIAN, BYE, and SMITH, CIRCUIT JUDGES, join, dissenting.

... Our panel opinion in this case, *see United States v. LeBrun,* 306 F.3d 545, 548–50, 552–56 (8th Cir.2002), very effectively rehearsed the tactics used to bring Mr. LeBrun to the point of confessing, which included threatening to ruin him financially, preying on fears related to his cancer, and vividly limning the effects that protracted civil and criminal litigation in a faraway place would have on his family, on its reputation, and in particular on his pregnant wife. I will therefore content myself with some observations on the court's opinion....

While, as the court notes, the agents never shouted at Mr. LeBrun or threatened him physically, the district court found on ample evidence that the atmosphere at the interrogation was police-dominated and that the agents frequently raised their voices and changed their tone when doing so. They also interrupted Mr. LeBrun in a bullying manner and demonstrated a threatening kind of impatience with him....

The court ... adverts to the fact that the district court made no findings as to what promises the interrogators actually made, but instead found only that Mr. LeBrun reasonably believed that he was promised that he would not be prosecuted if he would say that he had killed Mr. Muns "spontaneously." The court then looks for support in cases that hold that a mistaken belief as to what the law is will not render a confession involuntary. But in at least one of those, *Winfrey v. Wyrick,* 836 F.2d 406, 411–12 (8th Cir.1987), it was crucial to the holding that the defendant's mistaken belief that he would not be prosecuted was not induced by anything that his interviewers told him; it was based entirely on his own ideas about what the law was. I agree that that kind of mistake cannot possibly render a confession inadmissible. But the clear purport of what the agents said in this case was that Mr. LeBrun would not be prosecuted if he said what the agents wanted him to say, and they even assured Mr. LeBrun that Mr. Muns's family approved of the deal. Indeed, they said that the family would not pursue civil remedies if he confessed and apologized. What the family wanted, the interrogators said, was simply to clear Mr. Muns's name.

In addition to the part of the interview that the court quotes in its opinion, the record reveals that, both before and after the exchange that the court isolates, the interviewers made reference to an alleged statute of limitations difficulty that would prevent prosecution for a "spontaneous" murder; and the officers intimated, moreover, that if Mr. LeBrun would simply admit to a spontaneous killing, they would call the United States Attorney in charge of the prosecution and tell him that there was no case against Mr. LeBrun. In addition, I respectfully suggest that the district court did not, as the court maintains, note that the agents qualified their representations by telling Mr. LeBrun that it was "only 'possible' "that he would not be prosecuted. In relevant part, the transcript of the interview reveals only that one of the agents said at one point that "it was possible, beyond possible" that no prosecution would take place if Mr. LeBrun would cooperate, which is significantly different from what the court asserts was said. Taken in their entirety, the agents' assurances, which operated both as representations of what the law was and as promises, were categorical.

The district court shrank from holding that an absolute promise not to prosecute was made, not because of this part of the exchange between Mr. LeBrun and his interrogators, but because the promise not to prosecute was fleetingly qualified at one point, by one agent, by the condition that Mr. LeBrun must be telling the truth that the killing was spontaneous before the government would refrain from prosecution. This transitory allusion to truth-telling does nothing to undermine the district court's factual finding that Mr. LeBrun believed that he would not be prosecuted. My own examination of the transcript and the video tape leaves little room for doubt that the agents were in fact making such a representation about the law and a promise that Mr. LeBrun would not be prosecuted, and indeed it appears that the entire interview was deliberately structured around this stratagem. But nothing in particular really turns on this point: The coercive effect, if any, of a reasonably perceived promise is exactly the same as that of an actual promise.

In addition to the coercive tactics that the court briefly rehearses, among the enlarged pictures displayed prominently on the wall of the small interrogation room was a picture of Mr. Muns's family at his gravesite. The agents, moreover, did not merely invent generic phantom witnesses to the killing; they contrived a bizarre tale of a suicide note implicating Mr. LeBrun, and even claimed that there were other witnesses to the killing who were so haunted that their lives had been ruined by what they had seen. These were all knowing falsehoods. None of this finds a place in the court's opinion. Finally, and perhaps most importantly, the court fails altogether to mention the district court's finding that, despite the agents' assurances, Mr. LeBrun did not feel free to leave as the interview progressed. This is a finding of fact that is supported by Mr. LeBrun's testimony and cannot be reasonably rejected as clearly erroneous. It is also a finding that weighs heavily in favor of the district court's conclusion that Mr. LeBrun's confession was involuntary.

This is probably the right juncture to observe that it is not immediately apparent why statements by interrogators that are untrue, and known to be false, are more "coercive" than statements that are true. Such techniques may be reprehensible, but that fact would not seem to contribute to their propensity to overwhelm the will. Perhaps it is enough simply to note that the Supreme Court has said that "[t]he fact that the police misrepresented the statements that [a witness] had made is . . . relevant," *Frazier v. Cupp,* 394 U.S. 731, 739, 89 S.Ct. 1420, 22 L.Ed.2d 684 (1969), in circumstances like the present ones. But we need also to consider the possibility that what lies at the bottom of these kinds of cases is not merely an aversion to something called coercion, but a general uneasiness about the fairness of admitting confessions that were induced by knowing, lurid falsehoods and unfulfilled promises, whether "coercive" or not. In fact, the Supreme Court has specifically said that "the admissibility of a confession turns as much on whether the techniques for extracting the statements . . . are compatible with a system that presumes innocence and assures that a conviction will not be secured by inquisitorial means as on whether the defendant's will was in fact overborne." *Miller v. Fenton,* 474 U.S. 104, 116, 106 S.Ct. 445, 88 L.Ed.2d 405 (1985).

In sum, a consideration of the evidence in this case, including the kinds of pressure that were brought to bear on Mr. LeBrun, the assurances of leniency that went unfulfilled, and the deceit that the interrogators practiced, leads me to the conclusion that his confession was illegally obtained and should have been suppressed. At the very least, it seems to me relatively plain that the government has not carried its burden, *see Lego v. Twomey,* 404 U.S. 477, 489, 92 S.Ct. 619, 30 L.Ed.2d 618 (1972), of showing that the relevant statements were voluntary.

I therefore respectfully dissent and would affirm the judgment of the district court. . . .

B. MIRANDA V. ARIZONA AND THE INTERPRETATION OF ITS REQUIREMENTS

2. INTERPRETATION OF MIRANDA REQUIREMENTS

c. THE REQUIRED WARNINGS

Page 144, add at the end of Note 7, (New Main Case and Note):

Missouri v. Seibert

Supreme Court of the United States, 2004.
___ U.S. ___, 124 S.Ct. 2601.

* * *

■ JUSTICE SOUTER announced the judgment of the Court and delivered an opinion, in which JUSTICE STEVENS, JUSTICE GINSBURG, and JUSTICE BREYER join.

This case tests a police protocol for custodial interrogation that calls for giving no warnings of the rights to silence and counsel until interrogation has produced a confession. Although such a statement is generally inadmissible, since taken in violation of *Miranda v. Arizona,(1966)*, the interrogating officer follows it with *Miranda* warnings and then leads the suspect to cover the same ground a second time. The question here is the admissibility of the repeated statement. Because this midstream recitation of warnings after interrogation and unwarned confession could not effectively comply with *Miranda*'s constitutional requirement, we hold that a statement repeated after a warning in such circumstances is inadmissible.

I

Respondent Patrice Seibert's 12–year-old son Jonathan had cerebral palsy, and when he died in his sleep she feared charges of neglect because of bedsores on his body. In her presence, two of her teenage sons and two of their friends devised a plan to conceal the facts surrounding Jonathan's death by incinerating his body in the course of burning the family's mobile home, in which they planned to leave Donald Rector, a mentally ill teenager living with the family, to avoid any appearance that Jonathan had been unattended. Seibert's son Darian and a friend set the fire, and Donald died.

Five days later, the police awakened Seibert at 3 a.m. at a hospital where Darian was being treated for burns. In arresting her, Officer Kevin Clinton followed instructions from Rolla, Missouri, officer Richard Hanrahan that he refrain from giving *Miranda* warnings. After Seibert had been taken to the police station and left alone in an interview room for 15 to 20 minutes, Hanrahan questioned her without *Miranda* warnings for 30 to 40 minutes, squeezing her arm and repeating "Donald was also to die in his sleep." After Seibert finally admitted she knew Donald was meant to die in the fire, she was given a 20–minute coffee and cigarette break. Officer Hanrahan then turned on a tape recorder, gave Seibert the *Miranda* warnings, and obtained a signed waiver of rights from her. He resumed the questioning with "Ok, 'trice, we've been talking for a little while about what happened on Wednesday the twelfth, haven't we?," and confronted her with her prewarning statements:

> Hanrahan: "Now, in discussion you told us, you told us that there was an understanding about Donald."
>
> Seibert: "Yes."
>
> Hanrahan: "Did that take place earlier that morning?"
>
> Seibert: "Yes."
>
> Hanrahan: "And what was the understanding about Donald?"
>
> Seibert: "If they could get him out of the trailer, to take him out of the trailer."
>
> Hanrahan: "And if they couldn't?"
>
> Seibert: "I, I never even thought about it. I just figured they would."
>
> Hanrahan: " 'Trice, didn't you tell me that he was supposed to die in his sleep?"
>
> Seibert: "If that would happen, 'cause he was on that new medicine, you know. . . ."
>
> Hanrahan: "The Prozac? And it makes him sleepy. So he was supposed to die in his sleep?"
>
> Seibert: "Yes."

After being charged with first-degree murder for her role in Donald's death, Seibert sought to exclude both her prewarning and postwarning statements. At the suppression hearing, Officer Hanrahan testified that he made a "conscious decision" to withhold *Miranda* warnings, thus resorting to an interrogation technique he had been taught: question first, then give the warnings, and then repeat the question "until I get the answer that she's already provided once." He acknowledged that Seibert's ultimate statement was "largely a repeat of information . . . obtained" prior to the warning.

The trial court suppressed the prewarning statement but admitted the responses given after the *Miranda* recitation. A jury convicted Seibert of second-degree murder.

* * *

In *Miranda*, we explained that the "voluntariness doctrine in the state cases . . . encompasses all interrogation practices which are likely to exert such pressure upon an individual as to disable him from making a free and rational choice," We appreciated the difficulty of judicial enquiry *post hoc* into the circumstances of a police interrogation, *Dickerson v. United States, (2000)*, and recognized that "the coercion inherent in custodial interrogation blurs the line between voluntary and involuntary statements, and thus heightens the risk" that the privilege against self-incrimination will not be observed. Hence our concern that the "traditional totality-of-the-circumstances" test posed an "unacceptably great" risk that involuntary custodial confessions would escape detection.

Accordingly, "to reduce the risk of a coerced confession and to implement the *Self-Incrimination Clause*," *Chavez v. Martinez, (2003)* (KENNEDY, J., concurring in part and dissenting in part), this Court in *Miranda* concluded that "the accused must be adequately and effectively apprised of his rights and the exercise of those rights must be fully honored," *384 U.S., at 467, 16 L. Ed. 2d 694, 86 S. Ct. 1602*. *Miranda* conditioned the admissibility at trial of any custodial confession on warning a suspect of his rights: failure to give the prescribed warnings and obtain a waiver of rights before custodial questioning generally requires exclusion of any statements obtained. Conversely, giving the warnings and getting a waiver has generally produced a virtual ticket of admissibility; maintaining that a statement is involuntary even though given after warnings and voluntary waiver of rights requires unusual stamina, and litigation over voluntariness tends to end with the finding of a valid waiver. See *Berkemer v. McCarty, (1984)* ("Cases in which a defendant can make a colorable argument that a self-incriminating statement was 'compelled' despite the fact that the law enforcement authorities adhered to the dictates of *Miranda* are rare"). To point out the obvious, this common consequence would not be common at all were it not that *Miranda* warnings are customarily given under circumstances allowing for a real choice between talking and remaining silent.

III

There are those, of course, who preferred the old way of doing things, giving no warnings and litigating the voluntariness of any statement in nearly every instance. In the aftermath of *Miranda*, Congress even passed a statute seeking to restore that old regime, *18 U.S.C. § 3501*, although the Act lay dormant for years until finally invoked and challenged in *Dickerson v. United States, Dickerson* reaffirmed *Miranda* and held that its constitutional character prevailed against the statute.

The technique of interrogating in successive, unwarned and warned phases raises a new challenge to *Miranda*. Although we have no statistics on the frequency of this practice, it is not confined to Rolla, Missouri. An officer of that police department testified that the strategy of withholding *Miranda* warnings until after interrogating and drawing out a confession was promoted not only by his own department, but by a national police training organization and other departments in which he had worked. Consistently with the officer's testimony, the Police Law Institute, for example, instructs that "officers may conduct a two-stage interrogation.... At any point during the pre-*Miranda* interrogation, usually after arrestees have confessed, officers may then read the *Miranda* warnings and ask for a waiver. If the arrestees waive their *Miranda* rights, officers will be able to repeat any *subsequent* incriminating statements later in court." Police Law Institute, Illinois Police Law Manual 83 (Jan. 2001–Dec. 2003), ... (hereinafter Police Law Manual) (emphasis in original).[1] The upshot of all this

1. Emphasizing the impeachment exception to the *Miranda* rule approved by this Court, *Harris v. New York, (1971)*, some training programs advise officers to omit *Miranda* warnings altogether or to continue questioning after the suspect invokes his rights. See, *e.g.*, Police Law Manual 83

advice is a question-first practice of some popularity, as one can see from the reported cases describing its use, sometimes in obedience to departmental policy.

It is not the case, of course, that law enforcement educators en masse are urging that *Miranda* be honored only in the breach. See, *e.g.*, C. O'Hara & G. O'Hara, Fundamentals of Criminal Investigation 133 (7th ed. 2003) (instructing police to give *Miranda* warnings before conducting custodial interrogation); F. Inbau, J. Reid, & J. Buckley, Criminal Interrogation and Confessions 221 (3d ed. 1986) (hereinafter Inbau, Reid, & Buckley) (same); John Reid & Associates, Interviewing & Interrogation: The Reid Technique 61 (1991) (same). Most police manuals do not advocate the question-first tactic, because they understand that *Oregon v. Elstad, 470 U.S. 298, 84 L. Ed. 2d 222, 105 S. Ct. 1285 (1985)*, involved an officer's good-faith failure to warn. See, *e.g.*, Inbau, Reid, & Buckley 241 (*Elstad*'s "facts as well as [its] specific holding" instruct that "where an interrogator has failed to administer the *Miranda* warnings in the mistaken belief that, under the circumstances of the particular case, the warnings were not required, ... corrective measures ... salvage an interrogation opportunity").

IV

When a confession so obtained is offered and challenged, attention must be paid to the conflicting objects of *Miranda* and question-first. *Miranda* addressed "interrogation practices ... likely ... to disable [an individual] from making a free and rational choice" about speaking, and held that a suspect must be "adequately and effectively" advised of the choice the Constitution guarantees. The object of question-first is to render *Miranda* warnings ineffective by waiting for a particularly opportune time to give them, after the suspect has already confessed.

Just as "no talismanic incantation [is] required to satisfy [*Miranda*'s] strictures," *California v. Prysock, 453 U.S. 355, 359, 69 L. Ed. 2d 696, 101 S. Ct. 2806 (1981) (per curiam),* it would be absurd to think that mere recitation of the litany suffices to satisfy *Miranda* in every conceivable circumstance. "The inquiry is simply whether the warnings reasonably 'convey to [a suspect] his rights as required by *Miranda*.' " *Duckworth v. Eagan, (1989)*. The threshold issue when interrogators question first and warn later is thus whether it would be reasonable to find that in these circumstances the warnings could function "effectively" as *Miranda* requires. Could the warnings effectively advise the suspect that he had a real choice about giving an admissible statement at that juncture? Could they

("There is no need to give a *Miranda* warning before asking questions if ... the answers given ... will not be required by the prosecutor during the prosecution's case-in-chief"); California Commission on Peace Officer Standards and Training, Video Training Programs for California Law Enforcement, Miranda: Post–Invocation Questioning (broadcast July 11, 1996) ("We ... have been encouraging you to continue to question a suspect after they've invoked their *Miranda* rights"); D. Zulawski & D. Wicklander, Practical Aspects of Interview and Interrogation 50–51 (2d ed. 2002) (describing the practice of "beachheading" as useful for impeachment purpose (emphasis deleted)). . . .

reasonably convey that he could choose to stop talking even if he had talked earlier? For unless the warnings could place a suspect who has just been interrogated in a position to make such an informed choice, there is no practical justification for accepting the formal warnings as compliance with *Miranda*, or for treating the second stage of interrogation as distinct from the first, unwarned and inadmissible segment.

There is no doubt about the answer that proponents of question-first give to this question about the effectiveness of warnings given only after successful interrogation, and we think their answer is correct. By any objective measure, applied to circumstances exemplified here, it is likely that if the interrogators employ the technique of withholding warnings until after interrogation succeeds in eliciting a confession, the warnings will be ineffective in preparing the suspect for successive interrogation, close in time and similar in content. After all, the reason that question-first is catching on is as obvious as its manifest purpose, which is to get a confession the suspect would not make if he understood his rights at the outset; the sensible underlying assumption is that with one confession in hand before the warnings, the interrogator can count on getting its duplicate, with trifling additional trouble. Upon hearing warnings only in the aftermath of interrogation and just after making a confession, a suspect would hardly think he had a genuine right to remain silent, let alone persist in so believing once the police began to lead him over the same ground again. A more likely reaction on a suspect's part would be perplexity about the reason for discussing rights at that point, bewilderment being an unpromising frame of mind for knowledgeable decision. What is worse, telling a suspect that "anything you say can and will be used against you," without expressly excepting the statement just given, could lead to an entirely reasonable inference that what he has just said will be used, with subsequent silence being of no avail. Thus, when *Miranda* warnings are inserted in the midst of coordinated and continuing interrogation, they are likely to mislead and "deprive a defendant of knowledge essential to his ability to understand the nature of his rights and the consequences of abandoning them." *Moran v. Burbine, (1986).* By the same token, it would ordinarily be unrealistic to treat two spates of integrated and proximately conducted questioning as independent interrogations subject to independent evaluation simply because *Miranda* warnings formally punctuate them in the middle.

V

Missouri argues that a confession repeated at the end of an interrogation sequence envisioned in a question-first strategy is admissible on the authority of *Oregon v. Elstad, (1985)*, but the argument disfigures that case. In *Elstad*, the police went to the young suspect's house to take him into custody on a charge of burglary. Before the arrest, one officer spoke with the suspect's mother, while the other one joined the suspect in a "brief stop in the living room," where the officer said he "felt" the young man was involved in a burglary. The suspect acknowledged he had been at the scene. *Ibid.* This Court noted that the pause in the living room "was not to interrogate the suspect but to notify his mother of the reason for his arrest," and described the incident as having "none of the earmarks of coercion," The Court, indeed, took care to mention that the officer's initial failure to warn was an "oversight" that "may have been the result of confusion as to whether the brief exchange qualified as 'custodial interrogation' or ... may simply have reflected ... reluctance to initiate an alarming police procedure before [an officer] had spoken with respondent's mother." At the outset of a later and systematic station house interrogation going well beyond the scope of the laconic prior admission, the suspect was given *Miranda* warnings and made a full confession. In holding the second statement admissible and voluntary, *Elstad* rejected the "cat out of the bag" theory that any short, earlier admission, obtained in arguably innocent neglect of *Miranda*, determined the character of the later, warned confession, *Elstad, 470 U.S., at 311–314, 84 L. Ed. 2d 222, 105 S. Ct. 1285*; on the facts of that case, the Court thought any causal connection between the first and second responses to the police was "speculative and attenuated," Although the *Elstad* Court expressed no explicit conclusion about either officer's state of mind, it is fair to read *Elstad* as treating the living room conversation as a good-faith *Miranda* mistake, not only open to correction by careful warnings before systematic questioning in that particular case, but posing no threat to warn-first practice generally. See *Elstad, supra, at 309, 84 L. Ed. 2d 222, 105 S. Ct. 1285* (characterizing the officers' omission of *Miranda* warnings as "a simple failure to administer the warnings, unaccompanied by any actual coercion or other circumstances calculated to undermine the suspect's ability to exercise his free will"); (Justice Brennan's concern in dissent that *Elstad* would invite question-first practice "distorts the reasoning and holding of our decision, but, worse, invites trial courts and prosecutors to do the same").

The contrast between *Elstad* and this case reveals a series of relevant facts that bear on whether *Miranda* warnings delivered midstream could be effective enough to accomplish their object: the completeness and detail of the questions and answers in the first round of interrogation, the overlapping content of the two statements, the timing and setting of the first and the second, the continuity of police personnel, and the degree to which the interrogator's questions treated the second round as continuous with the first. In *Elstad*, it was not unreasonable to see the occasion for questioning at the station house as presenting a markedly different experience from the short conversation at home; since a reasonable person in the suspect's shoes could have seen the station house questioning as a new and distinct experience, the *Miranda* warnings could have made sense as presenting a genuine choice whether to follow up on the earlier admission.

At the opposite extreme are the facts here, which by any objective measure reveal a police strategy adapted to undermine the *Miranda* warnings.[2] The unwarned interrogation was conducted in the station house, and the questioning was systematic, exhaustive, and managed with psychological skill. When the police were finished there was little, if anything, of incriminating potential left unsaid. The warned phase of questioning proceeded after a pause of only 15 to 20 minutes, in the same place as the

2. Because the intent of the officer will rarely be as candidly admitted as it was here (even as it is likely to determine the conduct of the interrogation), the focus is on facts apart from intent that show the question-first tactic at work.

unwarned segment. When the same officer who had conducted the first phase recited the *Miranda* warnings, he said nothing to counter the probable misimpression that the advice that anything Seibert said could be used against her also applied to the details of the inculpatory statement previously elicited. In particular, the police did not advise that her prior statement could not be used.[3] Nothing was said or done to dispel the oddity of warning about legal rights to silence and counsel right after the police had led her through a systematic interrogation, and any uncertainty on her part about a right to stop talking about matters previously discussed would only have been aggravated by the way Officer Hanrahan set the scene by saying "we've been talking for a little while about what happened on Wednesday the twelfth, haven't we?" The impression that the further questioning was a mere continuation of the earlier questions and responses was fostered by references back to the confession already given. It would have been reasonable to regard the two sessions as parts of a continuum, in which it would have been unnatural to refuse to repeat at the second stage what had been said before. These circumstances must be seen as challenging the comprehensibility and efficacy of the *Miranda* warnings to the point that a reasonable person in the suspect's shoes would not have understood them to convey a message that she retained a choice about continuing to talk.

VI

Strategists dedicated to draining the substance out of *Miranda* cannot accomplish by training instructions what *Dickerson* held Congress could not do by statute. Because the question-first tactic effectively threatens to thwart *Miranda*'s purpose of reducing the risk that a coerced confession would be admitted, and because the facts here do not reasonably support a conclusion that the warnings given could have served their purpose, Seibert's postwarning statements are inadmissible. The judgment of the Supreme Court of Missouri is affirmed.

It is so ordered.

■ JUSTICE BREYER, concurring.

In my view, the following simple rule should apply to the two-stage interrogation technique: Courts should exclude the "fruits" of the initial unwarned questioning unless the failure to warn was in good faith. I believe this is a sound and workable approach to the problem this case presents. Prosecutors and judges have long understood how to apply the "fruits" approach, which they use in other areas of law. See *Wong Sun v. United States, (1963)*. And in the workaday world of criminal law enforcement the administrative simplicity of the familiar has significant advantages over a more complex exclusionary rule.

I believe the plurality's approach in practice will function as a "fruits" test. The truly "effective" *Miranda* warnings on which the plurality insists,

3. We do not hold that a formal addendum warning that a previous statement could not be used would be sufficient to change the character of the question-first procedure to the point of rendering an ensuing statement admissible, but its absence is clearly a factor that blunts the efficacy of the warnings and points to a continuing, not a new, interrogation.

will occur only when certain circumstances—a lapse in time, a change in location or interrogating officer, or a shift in the focus of the questioning—intervene between the unwarned questioning and any postwarning statement. Cf. *Taylor v. Alabama, (1982)* (evidence obtained subsequent to a constitutional violation must be suppressed as "fruit of the poisonous tree" unless "intervening events break the causal connection").

I consequently join the plurality's opinion in full. I also agree with *JUSTICE KENNEDY'S* opinion insofar as it is consistent with this approach and makes clear that a good-faith exception applies.

■ JUSTICE KENNEDY, concurring in the judgment.

The interrogation technique used in this case is designed to circumvent *Miranda v. Arizona, (1966)*. It undermines the *Miranda* warning and obscures its meaning. The plurality opinion is correct to conclude that statements obtained through the use of this technique are inadmissible....

... Not every violation of the rule requires suppression of the evidence obtained. Evidence is admissible when the central concerns of *Miranda* are not likely to be implicated and when other objectives of the criminal justice system are best served by its introduction. Thus, we have held that statements obtained in violation of the rule can be used for impeachment, so that the truth finding function of the trial is not distorted by the defense, see *Harris v. New York, (1971)*; that there is an exception to protect countervailing concerns of public safety, see *New York v. Quarles, (1984)*; and that physical evidence obtained in reliance on statements taken in violation of the rule is admissible, see *United States* v. *Patane*. These cases, in my view, are correct. They recognize that admission of evidence is proper when it would further important objectives without compromising *Miranda*'s central concerns. Under these precedents, the scope of the *Miranda* suppression remedy depends on a consideration of those legitimate interests and on whether admission of the evidence under the circumstances would frustrate *Miranda*'s central concerns and objectives.

* * *

In my view, *Elstad* was correct in its reasoning and its result. *Elstad* reflects a balanced and pragmatic approach to enforcement of the *Miranda* warning. An officer may not realize that a suspect is in custody and warnings are required. The officer may not plan to question the suspect or may be waiting for a more appropriate time. Skilled investigators often interview suspects multiple times, and good police work may involve referring to prior statements to test their veracity or to refresh recollection. In light of these realities it would be extravagant to treat the presence of one statement that cannot be admitted under *Miranda* as sufficient reason to prohibit subsequent statements preceded by a proper warning....

This case presents different considerations. The police used a two-step questioning technique based on a deliberate violation of *Miranda*. The *Miranda* warning was withheld to obscure both the practical and legal significance of the admonition when finally given. As JUSTICE SOUTER points out, the two-step technique permits the accused to conclude that the right not to respond did not exist when the earlier incriminating statements were made. The strategy is based on the assumption that *Miranda* warnings will tend to mean less when recited midinterrogation, after inculpatory statements have already been obtained. This tactic relies on an intentional misrepresentation of the protection that *Miranda* offers and does not serve any legitimate objectives that might otherwise justify its use.

Further, the interrogating officer here relied on the defendant's prewarning statement to obtain the postwarning statement used against her at trial. The postwarning interview resembled a cross-examination. The officer confronted the defendant with her inadmissible prewarning statements and pushed her to acknowledge them. See App. 70 (" 'Trice, didn't you tell me that he was supposed to die in his sleep?"). This shows the temptations for abuse inherent in the two-step technique. Reference to the prewarning statement was an implicit suggestion that the mere repetition of the earlier statement was not independently incriminating. The implicit suggestion was false.

* * *

The plurality concludes that whenever a two-stage interview occurs, admissibility of the postwarning statement should depend on "whether the *Miranda* warnings delivered midstream could have been effective enough to accomplish their object" given the specific facts of the case. This test envisions an objective inquiry from the perspective of the suspect, and applies in the case of both intentional and unintentional two-stage interrogations. In my view, this test cuts too broadly. *Miranda*'s clarity is one of its strengths, and a multifactor test that applies to every two-stage interrogation may serve to undermine that clarity. I would apply a narrower test applicable only in the infrequent case, such as we have here, in which the two-step interrogation technique was used in a calculated way to undermine the *Miranda* warning.

The admissibility of postwarning statements should continue to be governed by the principles of *Elstad* unless the deliberate two-step strategy was employed. If the deliberate two-step strategy has been used, postwarning statements that are related to the substance of prewarning statements must be excluded unless curative measures are taken before the postwarning statement is made. Curative measures should be designed to ensure that a reasonable person in the suspect's situation would understand the import and effect of the *Miranda* warning and of the *Miranda* waiver. For example, a substantial break in time and circumstances between the prewarning statement and the *Miranda* warning may suffice in most circumstances, as it allows the accused to distinguish the two contexts and appreciate that the interrogation has taken a new turn. Alternatively, an additional warning that explains the likely inadmissibility of the prewarning custodial statement may be sufficient. No curative steps were taken in this case, however, so the postwarning statements are inadmissible and the conviction cannot stand.

For these reasons, I concur in the judgment of the Court.

■ JUSTICE O'CONNOR, with whom THE CHIEF JUSTICE, JUSTICE SCALIA, and JUSTICE THOMAS join, dissenting.

The plurality devours *Oregon v. Elstad, (1985)*, even as it accuses petitioner's argument of "disfiguring" that decision. I believe that we are bound by *Elstad* to reach a different result, and I would vacate the judgment of the Supreme Court of Missouri.

I

On two preliminary questions I am in full agreement with the plurality. First, the plurality appropriately follows *Elstad* in concluding that Seibert's statement cannot be held inadmissible under a "fruit of the poisonous tree" theory. Second, the plurality correctly declines to focus its analysis on the subjective intent of the interrogating officer.

A

This Court has made clear that there simply is no place for a robust deterrence doctrine with regard to violations of *Miranda v. Arizona, (1966).* See *Dickerson v. United States, (2000)* ("Our decision in *[Elstad]*—refusing to apply the traditional 'fruits' doctrine developed in *Fourth Amendment* cases— . . . simply recognizes the fact that unreasonable searches under the *Fourth Amendment* are different from unwarned interrogation under the *Fifth Amendment*"); *Elstad, supra, at 306, 84 L. Ed. 2d 222, 105 S. Ct. 1285* (unlike the *Fourth Amendment* exclusionary rule, the "*Miranda* exclusionary rule . . . serves the *Fifth Amendment* and sweeps more broadly than the *Fifth Amendment* itself") . . . .

Although the analysis the plurality ultimately espouses examines the same facts and circumstances that a "fruits" analysis would consider (such as the lapse of time between the two interrogations and change of questioner or location), it does so for entirely different reasons. The fruits analysis would examine those factors because they are relevant to the balance of deterrence value versus the "drastic and socially costly course" of excluding reliable evidence. *Nix v. Williams, (1984).* The plurality, by contrast, looks to those factors to inform the *psychological* judgment regarding whether the suspect has been informed effectively of her right to remain silent. The analytical underpinnings of the two approaches are thus entirely distinct, and they should not be conflated just because they function similarly in practice.

B

The plurality's rejection of an intent-based test is also, in my view, correct. Freedom from compulsion lies at the heart of the *Fifth Amendment*, and requires us to assess whether a suspect's decision to speak truly was voluntary. Because voluntariness is a matter of the suspect's state of mind, we focus our analysis on the way in which suspects experience interrogation . . . .

Thoughts kept inside a police officer's head cannot affect that experience. See *Moran v. Burbine, (1986)* ("Events occurring outside of the presence of the suspect and entirely unknown to him surely can have no bearing on the capacity to comprehend and knowingly relinquish a constitutional right") . . . . A suspect who experienced the exact same interrogation as Seibert, save for a difference in the undivulged, subjective intent of the interrogating officer when he failed to give *Miranda* warnings, would not experience the interrogation any differently . . . .

Because the isolated fact of Officer Hanrahan's intent could not have had any bearing on Seibert's "capacity to comprehend and knowingly relinquish" her right to remain silent, *Moran, 89 L. Ed. 2d 410, 106 S. Ct. 1135*, it could not by itself affect the voluntariness of her confession. Moreover, recognizing an exception to *Elstad* for intentional violations would require focusing constitutional analysis on a police officer's subjective intent, an unattractive proposition that we all but uniformly avoid. In general, "we believe that 'sending state and federal courts on an expedition into the minds of police officers would produce a grave and fruitless misallocation of judicial resources.' " *United States v. Leon, (1984).* This case presents the uncommonly straightforward circumstance of an officer openly admitting that the violation was intentional. But the inquiry will be complicated in other situations probably more likely to occur. For example, different officers involved in an interrogation might claim different states of mind regarding the failure to give *Miranda* warnings. Even in the simple case of a single officer who claims that a failure to give *Miranda* warnings was inadvertent, the likelihood of error will be high. See W. LaFave, Search and Seizure § 1.4(e), p. 124 (3d ed. 1996) ("There is no reason to believe that courts can with any degree of success determine in which instances the police had an ulterior motive").

These evidentiary difficulties have led us to reject an intent-based test in several criminal procedure contexts. For example, in *New York v. Quarles, (1984)*, one of the factors that led us to reject an inquiry into the subjective intent of the police officer in crafting a test for the "public safety" exception to *Miranda* was that officers' motives will be "largely unverifiable." Similarly, our opinion in *Whren v. United States, (1996)*, made clear that "the evidentiary difficulty of establishing subjective intent" was one of the reasons (albeit not the principal one) for refusing to consider intent in *Fourth Amendment* challenges generally.

For these reasons, I believe that the approach espoused by JUSTICE KENNEDY is ill advised.... This approach untethers the analysis from facts knowable to, and therefore having any potential directly to affect, the suspect. Far from promoting "clarity," *ibid.*, the approach will add a third step to the suppression inquiry. In virtually every two-stage interrogation case, in addition to addressing the standard *Miranda* and voluntariness questions, courts will be forced to conduct the kind of difficult, state-of-mind inquiry that we normally take pains to avoid.

II

The plurality's adherence to *Elstad*, and mine to the plurality, end there. Our decision in *Elstad* rejected the ... argument that the "lingering compulsion" inherent in a defendant's having let the "cat out of the bag" required suppression....

We rejected this theory outright. We did so not because we refused to recognize the "psychological impact of the suspect's conviction that he has let the cat out of the bag," but because we refused to "endow" those "psychological effects" with "constitutional implications." To do so, we said, would "effectively immunize a suspect who responds to pre-*Miranda* warning questions from the consequences of his subsequent informed waiver,'' an immunity that ''comes at a high cost to legitimate law enforcement activity, while adding little desirable protection to the individual's interest in not being *compelled* to testify against himself.'' *84 L.Ed. 2d 222, 105 S. Ct. 1285*. The plurality might very well think that we struck the balance between *Fifth Amendment* rights and law enforcement interests incorrectly in *Elstad;* but that is not normally a sufficient reason for ignoring the dictates of *stare decisis*.

I would analyze the two-step interrogation procedure under the voluntariness standards central to the *Fifth Amendment* and reiterated in *Elstad*. *Elstad* commands that if Seibert's first statement is shown to have been involuntary, the court must examine whether the taint dissipated through the passing of time or a change in circumstances: ''When a prior statement is actually coerced, the time that passes between confessions, the change in place of interrogations, and the change in identity of the interrogators all bear on whether that coercion has carried over into the second confession.'' In addition, Seibert's second statement should be suppressed if she showed that it was involuntary despite the *Miranda* warnings. . . . Although I would leave this analysis for the Missouri courts to conduct on remand, I note that, unlike the officers in *Elstad*, Officer Hanrahan referred to Seibert's unwarned statement during the second part of the interrogation when she made a statement at odds with her unwarned confession. ('' 'Trice, didn't you tell me that he was supposed to die in his sleep?'') . . . . Such a tactic may bear on the voluntariness inquiry. . . .

* * *

Because I believe that the plurality gives insufficient deference to *Elstad* and that JUSTICE KENNEDY places improper weight on subjective intent, I respectfully dissent.

NOTE

Does Missouri v. Seibert change the prevailing rules (See p. 97–101) governing deliberate attempts to avoid Miranda by conducting non-custodial interviews?

CHAPTER 4

WIRETAPPING AND ELECTRONIC SURVEILLANCE

B. NON-CONSENSUAL WIRETAPPING AND ELECTRONIC SURVEILLANCE

Add to note 3 on page 331:

Congress later prohibited the installation of a pen register without a court order. 18 U.S. C. § 3121(a). Evidence obtained through the illegal installation of a pen register is still admissible in a criminal trial, however, since the seized evidence is seized in violation of a statute and not in violation of the Fourth Amendment constitutional provisions. United States v. Thompson, 936 F.2d 1249 (11th Cir. 1991), *cert. denied*, 502 U.S. 1075, 112 S.Ct. 975 (1992).

In the past this statute authorized a judge in a court with jurisdiction over the crime to enter an order to permit a pen register or a trap and trace device that could be used only in that jurisdiction. 18 U.S.C. § 1323 (2000 ed.). Now, the Patriot Act permits the government to apply to a court with jurisdiction over the crime for an order that may be used anywhere in the United States 18 U.S.C. §§ 3123 (B)(1)(c), 3127(2).

Add to note 4 on page 331:

Professor Orin Kerr has written about the survival of the property paradigm after *Katz*. Orin G. Kerr, "The Fourth Amendment in New Technologies: Constitutional Myths and the Case for Restraint," ___ Michigan L. Rev. ___ (2004). See also Swire, Peter P. "*Katz* is Dead, Long Live *Katz*," ___ Mich. L. Rev. ___ (2004) forthcoming http://ssrn.com/abstract=490623.

Add to note 9 on page 347:

In 2003, courts issued 1,442 authorizations for intercept orders as a result of 578 federal applications and 864 state applications. This represents an increase of 6% over the number issued in 2003. The increase occurred in federal orders which rose 16% in number as compared to the number of state orders which rose only .03%. As in prior years, the most common type of case for which intercepts were sought were those cases involving narcotics and drug trafficking. As in prior years, the risk of rejection was low. In 2004, 1,442 authorizations were sought and 1,442 were issued. None were refused, though a number were amended and not all were installed. 2003 Report of the Director of the Administrative Office of the United States Courts on applications for Orders Authorizing or Approving the Interception of Wire, Oral or Electronic Communications http://www.uscourts.gov/wiretap03/contents.html.

CHAPTER 5

The Law of Arrest, Search and Seizure

B. Probable Cause

Add note 3(d) to the end of note 3 on page 409:

(d) How specific does the probable cause have to be? Suppose officers have clear probable cause to believe a crime has been committed, but it is unclear which, if any, of multiple suspects committed it?

How does an officer measure probable cause when multiple parties are involved? The United States Supreme Court addressed this question in Maryland v. Pringle, ___ U.S. ___, 124 S.Ct. 795 (2003). There, officers pulled over a passenger car in the early morning hours for speeding. There were three occupants in the car, two in front and one in the back seat. A consent search turned up $763 in the front glove compartment and five glassine baggies of cocaine between the back seat and the back seat armrest. When none of the occupants claimed ownership of the drugs, the officers placed all three under arrest. Later defendant Pringle, who had been the front seat passenger, confessed (after waiving his *Miranda* rights) and claimed ownership of the contraband. He moved to suppress his confession as the fruit of an illegal arrest, arguing that the officers lacked probable cause to arrest him. The trial court denied his motion and he was convicted and sentenced to 10 years incarceration.

On appeal, his conviction was reversed by a divided court. The Court of Appeals of Maryland held that "there was not probable cause to arrest petitioner, who was not the owner of the vehicle, when petitioner was merely the front seat passenger and the only evidence supporting the arrest was a sum of money in the closed front glove compartment and drugs that were hidden from view in the armrest in the backseat of the vehicle." 370 Md. 525, 531, 805 A.2d 1016, 1019 (2002).

The United States Supreme Court disagreed and held that the arresting officer did have sufficient probable cause. First, all agreed that on these facts, the discovery of the illegal drugs constituted unquestionable probable cause to believe a crime had been committed. There was only the issue of whether there was sufficient probable cause that this defendant had committed it. Relying on Wyoming v. Houghton, 526 U.S. 295, 119 S.Ct. 1297 (1999), the Court found that it was reasonable for the officer to have inferred a common criminal enterprise in this situation. The Court rejected the defendant's argument based on Ybarra v. Illinois, 444 U.S. 85, 100 S.Ct. 338 (1979) that "mere propinquity" was not enough.

C. The Issuance of Warrants

Add to note 3 on page 412:

In *Groh v. Ramirez*, 540 U.S. ___ , 124 S.Ct. 1284 (2004), although the affidavit in support of the warrant set forth probable cause, the warrant itself lacked particularity and did not describe the items to be seized at all. The agent inserted a description of the place to be searched in the warrant space provided for the items to be seized. Thus, no items were listed in the warrant itself. The Supreme Court held that the search violated the Fourth Amendment. The Court further determined on these facts that the agent was not entitled to a good faith defense and further, the agent would not receive qualified immunity in this civil action for the violation of constitutional rights.

E. THE LAW OF ARREST AND OF SEARCH INCIDENT TO ARREST

Add in new paragraph at end of quote from New York v. Belton, 453 U.S. 454, 101 S.Ct. 2860 (1981) in section on *Special Rules for Searches Beyond the Person of Motor Vehicle Driver or Passenger Arrestees* on page 444:

The United States Supreme Court has further expanded the search incident to arrest exception when vehicles are involved:

Thornton v. United States

___ U.S. ___, 124 S.Ct. 2127 (May 24, 2004).

■ JUDGES: REHNQUIST, C. J., delivered the opinion of the Court except as to footnote 4. KENNEDY, THOMAS, and BREYER, JJ., joined that opinion in full, and O'CONNOR, J., joined as to all but footnote 4. O'CONNOR, J., filed an opinion concurring in part. SCALIA, J., filed an opinion concurring in the judgment, in which GINSBURG, J., joined. STEVENS, J., filed a dissenting opinion, in which SOUTER, J., joined.

■ OPINION: CHIEF JUSTICE REHNQUIST delivered the opinion of the Court except as to footnote 4.

In *New York* v. *Belton,* 453 U.S. 454, 101 S. Ct. 2860 (1981), we held that when a police officer has made a lawful custodial arrest of an occupant of an automobile, the Fourth Amendment allows the officer to search the passenger compartment of that vehicle as a contemporaneous incident of arrest. We have granted certiorari twice before to determine whether *Belton*'s rule is limited to situations where the officer makes contact with the occupant while the occupant is inside the vehicle, or whether it applies as well when the officer first makes contact with the arrestee after the latter has stepped out of his vehicle. We did not reach the merits in either of those two cases. Arizona v. Gant, 540 U.S. ___, 124 S. Ct. 461 (2003) (vacating and remanding for reconsideration in light of State v. Dean, 206 Ariz. 158, 76 P. 3d 429 (2003)); *Florida* v. *Thomas,* 532 U.S. 774, 121 S. Ct. 1905 (2001) (dismissing for lack of jurisdiction). We now reach that question and conclude that *Belton* governs even when an officer does not make contact until the person arrested has left the vehicle.

Officer Deion Nichols of the Norfolk, Virginia, Police Department, who was in uniform but driving an unmarked police car, first noticed petitioner Marcus Thornton when petitioner slowed down so as to avoid driving next to him. Nichols suspected that petitioner knew he was a police officer and for some reason did not want to pull next to him. His suspicions aroused,

Nichols pulled off onto a side street and petitioner passed him. After petitioner passed him, Nichols ran a check on petitioner's license tags, which revealed that the tags had been issued to a 1982 Chevy two-door and not to a Lincoln Town Car, the model of car petitioner was driving. Before Nichols had an opportunity to pull him over, petitioner drove into a parking lot, parked, and got out of the vehicle. Nichols saw petitioner leave his vehicle as he pulled in behind him. He parked the patrol car, accosted petitioner, and asked him for his driver's license. He also told him that his license tags did not match the vehicle that he was driving.

Petitioner appeared nervous. He began rambling and licking his lips; he was sweating. Concerned for his safety, Nichols asked petitioner if he had any narcotics or weapons on him or in his vehicle. Petitioner said no. Nichols then asked petitioner if he could pat him down, to which petitioner agreed. Nichols felt a bulge in petitioner's left front pocket and again asked him if he had any illegal narcotics on him. This time petitioner stated that he did, and he reached into his pocket and pulled out two individual bags, one containing three bags of marijuana and the other containing a large amount of crack cocaine. Nichols handcuffed petitioner, informed him that he was under arrest, and placed him in the back seat of the patrol car. He then searched petitioner's vehicle and found a BryCo .9–millimeter handgun under the driver's seat.

A grand jury charged petitioner with possession with intent to distribute cocaine base, 84 Stat. 1260, 21 U.S.C. § 841(a)(1), possession of a firearm after having been previously convicted of a crime punishable by a term of imprisonment exceeding one year, 18 U.S.C. § 922(g)(1), and possession of a firearm in furtherance of a drug trafficking crime, § 924(c)(1). Petitioner sought to suppress, *inter alia*, the firearm as the fruit of an unconstitutional search. After a hearing, the District Court denied petitioner's motion to suppress, holding that the automobile search was valid under *New York* v. *Belton, supra,* and alternatively that Nichols could have conducted an inventory search of the automobile. A jury convicted petitioner on all three counts; he was sentenced to 180 months' imprisonment and 8 years of supervised release.

Petitioner appealed, challenging only the District Court's denial of the suppression motion. He argued that *Belton* was limited to situations where the officer initiated contact with an arrestee while he was still an occupant of the car. The United States Court of Appeals for the Fourth Circuit affirmed. 325 F.3d 189 (2003). It held that "the historical rationales for the search incident to arrest doctrine—'the need to disarm the suspect in order to take him into custody' and 'the need to preserve evidence for later use at trial,' " *id.*, at 195 (quoting *Knowles* v. *Iowa,* 525 U.S. 113, 116, 119 S. Ct. 484 (1998)), did not require *Belton* to be limited solely to situations in which suspects were still in their vehicles when approached by the police. Noting that petitioner conceded that he was in "close proximity, both temporally and spatially," to his vehicle, the court concluded that the car was within petitioner's immediate control, and thus Nichols' search was reasonable under *Belton*.[1] 325 F.3d at 196. We granted certiorari, 540 U.S. ___, 124 S. Ct. 461 (2003), and now affirm.

1. The Court of Appeals did not reach the District Court's alternative holding that Nichols could have conducted a lawful inventory search. 325 F.3d at 196.

In *Belton*, an officer overtook a speeding vehicle on the New York Thruway and ordered its driver to pull over (cites omitted). Suspecting that the occupants possessed marijuana, the officer directed them to get out of the car and arrested them for unlawful possession. He searched them and then searched the passenger compartment of the car. We considered the constitutionally permissible scope of a search in these circumstances and sought to lay down a workable rule governing that situation.

We first referred to *Chimel* v. *California,* 395 U.S. 752, 89 S. Ct. 2034 (1969), a case where the arrestee was arrested in his home, and we had described the scope of a search incident to a lawful arrest as the person of the arrestee and the area immediately surrounding him (cites omitted) This rule was justified by the need to remove any weapon the arrestee might seek to use to resist arrest or to escape, and the need to prevent the concealment or destruction of evidence (cite omitted). Although easily stated, the *Chimel* principle had proved difficult to apply in specific cases. We pointed out that in *United States* v. *Robinson,* 414 U.S. 218, 94 S. Ct. 467 (1973), a case dealing with the scope of the search of the arrestee's person, we had rejected a suggestion that " 'there must be litigated in each case the issue of whether or not there was present one of the reasons supporting the authority' " to conduct such a search (cite omitted). Similarly, because "courts had found no workable definition of the 'area within the immediate control of the arrestee' when that area arguably included the interior of an automobile and the arrestee was its recent occupant," (cite omitted), we sought to set forth a clear rule for police officers and citizens alike. We therefore held that "when a policeman has made a lawful custodial arrest of the occupant of an automobile, he may, as a contemporaneous incident of that arrest, search the passenger compartment of that automobile." (footnotes omitted).

In so holding, we placed no reliance on the fact that the officer in *Belton* ordered the occupants out of the vehicle, or initiated contact with them while they remained within it. Nor do we find such a factor persuasive in distinguishing the current situation, as it bears no logical relationship to *Belton*'s rationale. There is simply no basis to conclude that the span of the area generally within the arrestee's immediate control is determined by whether the arrestee exited the vehicle at the officer's direction, or whether the officer initiated contact with him while he remained in the car. We recognized as much, albeit in dicta, in *Michigan* v. *Long,* (cite omitted), where officers observed a speeding car swerve into a ditch. The driver exited and the officers met him at the rear of his car. Although there was no indication that the officers initiated contact with the driver while he was still in the vehicle, we observed that "it is clear ... that if the officers had arrested [respondent] ... they could have searched the passenger compartment under *New York* v. *Belton.*" (cite omitted).

In all relevant aspects, the arrest of a suspect who is next to a vehicle presents identical concerns regarding officer safety and the destruction of evidence as the arrest of one who is inside the vehicle. An officer may search a suspect's vehicle under *Belton* only if the suspect is arrested (cite omitted). A custodial arrest is fluid and "the danger to the police officer flows from *the fact of the arrest*, and its attendant proximity, stress, and uncertainty," *Robinson, supra*,(cites omitted). (emphasis added). See *Washington* v. *Chrisman,* 455 U.S. 1, 7, 102 S. Ct. 812 (1982) ("Every arrest must be presumed to present a risk of danger to the arresting officer"). The stress is no less merely because the arrestee exited his car before the officer initiated contact, nor is an arrestee less likely to attempt to lunge for a weapon or to destroy evidence if he is outside of, but still in control of, the vehicle. In either case, the officer faces a highly volatile situation. It would make little sense to apply two different rules to what is, at bottom, the same situation.

In some circumstances it may be safer and more effective for officers to conceal their presence from a suspect until he has left his vehicle. Certainly that is a judgment officers should be free to make. But under the strictures of petitioner's proposed "contact initiation" rule, officers who do so would be unable to search the car's passenger compartment in the event of a custodial arrest, potentially compromising their safety and placing incriminating evidence at risk of concealment or destruction. The Fourth Amendment does not require such a gamble.

Petitioner argues, however, that *Belton* will fail to provide a "bright-line" rule if it applies to more than vehicle "occupants." Brief for Petitioner 29–34. But *Belton* allows police to search the passenger compartment of a vehicle incident to a lawful custodial arrest of both "occupants" and "recent occupants" (cite omitted). Indeed, the respondent in *Belton* was not inside the car at the time of the arrest and search; he was standing on the highway. In any event, while an arrestee's status as a "recent occupant" may turn on his temporal or spatial relationship to the car at the time of the arrest and search,[2] it certainly does not turn on whether he was inside or outside the car at the moment that the officer first initiated contact with him.

To be sure, not all contraband in the passenger compartment is likely to be readily accessible to a "recent occupant." It is unlikely in this case that petitioner could have reached under the driver's seat for his gun once he was outside of his automobile. But the firearm and the passenger compartment in general were no more inaccessible than were the contraband and the passenger compartment in *Belton*. The need for a clear rule, readily understood by police officers and not depending on differing estimates of what items were or were not within reach of an arrestee at any particular moment, justifies the sort of generalization which *Belton* enunciated.[3]

2. Petitioner argues that if we reject his proposed "contact initiation" rule, we should limit the scope of *Belton* to "recent distance" of the car. Brief for Petitioner 35–26. We decline to address petitioner's argument, however, as it is outside the question on which we granted certiorari, (cite omitted)....

3. Justice Stevens contends that *Belton's* bright-line rule "is not needed for cases in which the arrestee is first accosted when he is a pedestrian, because *Chimel* [v. *California,* 395 U.S. 752, 89 S. Ct. 2034 (1969),] itself provides all the guidance that is necessary." (dissenting opinion). Under Justice Stevens' approach, however, even if the car itself was within the arrestee's reaching dis-

Once an officer determines that there is probable cause to make an arrest, it is reasonable to allow officers to ensure their safety and to preserve evidence by searching the entire passenger compartment.

Rather than clarifying the constitutional limits of a *Belton* search, petitioner's "contact initiation" rule would obfuscate them. Under petitioner's proposed rule, an officer approaching a suspect who has just alighted from his vehicle would have to determine whether he actually confronted or signaled confrontation with the suspect while he remained in the car, or whether the suspect exited his vehicle unaware of, and for reasons unrelated to, the officer's presence. This determination would be inherently subjective and highly fact specific, and would require precisely the sort of ad hoc determinations on the part of officers in the field and reviewing courts that *Belton* sought to avoid. (cite omitted). Experience has shown that such a rule is impracticable, and we refuse to adopt it. So long as an arrestee is the sort of "recent occupant" of a vehicle such as petitioner was here, officers may search that vehicle incident to the arrest.[4]

The judgment of the Court of Appeals is affirmed.

It is so ordered.

■ CONCUR: JUSTICE O'CONNOR, concurring in part

I join all but footnote 4 of the Court's opinion. Although the opinion is a logical extension of the holding of *New York* v. *Belton,* (cite omitted). I write separately to express my dissatisfaction with the state of the law in this area. As Justice Scalia forcefully argues, (opinion concurring in judgment), lower court decisions seem now to treat the ability to search a vehicle incident to the arrest of a recent occupant as a police entitlement rather than as an exception justified by the twin rationales of *Chimel* v. *California,* (cite omitted). That erosion is a direct consequence of *Belton*'s shaky foundation. While the approach Justice Scalia proposes appears to be

tance under *Chimel*, police officers and courts would still have to determine whether a particular object within the passenger compartment was also within an arrestee's reaching distance under *Chimel*. This is exactly the type of unworkable and fact-specific inquiry that *Belton* rejected by holding that the entire passenger compartment may be searched when " 'the area within the immediate control of the arrestee' . . . arguably includes the interior of an automobile and the arrestee is its recent occupant" (cite omitted).

4. Whatever the merits of Justice Scalia opinion concurring in the judgment, this is the wrong case in which to address them. Petitioner has never argued that *Belton* should be limited "to cases where it is reasonable to believe evidence relevant to the crime of arrest might be found in the vehicle," nor did any court below consider Justice Scalia's reasoning. See *Pennsylvania Dept. of Corrections* v. *Yeskey,* 524 U.S. 206, 212–213, 118 S. Ct. 1952 (1998) (" 'Where issues are neither raised before nor considered by the Court of Appeals, this Court will not ordinarily consider them' " (cite omitted).) The question presented—"whether the bright-line rule announced in *New York* v. *Belton* is confined to situations in which the police initiate contact with the occupant of a vehicle while that person is in the vehicle," Pet. for Cert.—does not fairly encompass Justice Scalia's analysis. See this Court's Rule 14.1(a) ("Only the questions set out in the petition, or fairly included therein, will be considered by the Court"). And the United States has never had an opportunity to respond to such an approach. See *Yee* v. *Escondido,* 503 U.S. 519, 536,112 S. Ct. 1522 (1992). Under these circumstances, it would be imprudent to overrule, for all intents and purposes, our established constitutional precedent, which governs police authority in a common occurrence such as automobile searches pursuant to arrest, and we decline to do so at this time.

built on firmer ground, I am reluctant to adopt it in the context of a case in which neither the Government nor the petitioner has had a chance to speak to its merit.

■ JUSTICE SCALIA, with whom JUSTICE GINSBURG joins, concurring in the judgment.

In *Chimel* v. *California,* (cite omitted), we held that a search incident to arrest was justified only as a means to find weapons the arrestee might use or evidence he might conceal or destroy. We accordingly limited such searches to the area within the suspect's " 'immediate control' "—*i.e.*, "the area into which an arrestee might reach in order to grab a weapon or evidentiary item" (cite omitted). In *New York* v. *Belton,*(cite omitted), we set forth a bright-line rule for arrests of automobile occupants, holding that, because the vehicle's entire passenger compartment is "in fact generally, even if not inevitably," within the arrestee's immediate control, a search of the whole compartment is justified in every case.

When petitioner's car was searched in this case, he was neither in, nor anywhere near, the passenger compartment of his vehicle. Rather, he was handcuffed and secured in the back of the officer's squad car. The risk that he would nevertheless "grab a weapon or evidentiary item" from his car was remote in the extreme. The Court's effort to apply our current doctrine to this search stretches it beyond its breaking point, and for that reason I cannot join the Court's opinion.

I

I see three reasons why the search in this case might have been justified to protect officer safety or prevent concealment or destruction of evidence. None ultimately persuades me.

The first is that, despite being handcuffed and secured in the back of a squad car, petitioner might have escaped and retrieved a weapon or evidence from his vehicle—a theory that calls to mind Judge Goldberg's reference to the mythical arrestee "possessed of the skill of Houdini and the strength of Hercules." *United States* v. *Frick*, 490 F.2d 666, 673 (CA5 1973) (opinion concurring in part and dissenting in part). The United States, endeavoring to ground this seemingly speculative fear in reality, points to a total of seven instances over the past 13 years in which state or federal officers were attacked with weapons by handcuffed or formerly handcuffed arrestees. (cite omitted). These instances do not, however, justify the search authority claimed. . . .

Of course, the Government need not document specific instances in order to justify measures that avoid obvious risks. But the risk here is far from obvious, and in a context as frequently recurring as roadside arrests, the Government's inability to come up with even a single example of a handcuffed arrestee's retrieval of arms or evidence from his vehicle undermines its claims. The risk that a suspect handcuffed in the back of a squad car might escape and recover a weapon from his vehicle is surely no greater than the risk that a suspect handcuffed in his residence might escape and recover a weapon from the next room—a danger we held insufficient to justify a search in *Chimel* (cite omitted).

The second defense of the search in this case is that, since the officer could have conducted the search at the time of arrest (when the suspect was still near the car), he should not be penalized for having taken the sensible precaution of securing the suspect in the squad car first. As one Court of Appeals put it: " 'It does not make sense to prescribe a constitutional test that is entirely at odds with safe and sensible police procedures' " (cites omitted). The weakness of this argument is that it assumes that, one way or another, the search must take place. But conducting a *Chimel* search is not the Government's right; it is an exception—justified by necessity—to a rule that would otherwise render the search unlawful. If "sensible police procedures" require that suspects be handcuffed and put in squad cars, then police should handcuff suspects, put them in squad cars, and not conduct the search. Indeed, if an officer leaves a suspect unrestrained nearby just to manufacture authority to search, one could argue that the search is unreasonable *precisely because* the dangerous conditions justifying it existed only by virtue of the officer's failure to follow sensible procedures.

The third defense of the search is that, even though the arrestee posed no risk here, *Belton* searches in general are reasonable, and the benefits of a bright-line rule justify upholding that small minority of searches that, on their particular facts, are not reasonable. The validity of this argument rests on the accuracy of *Belton*'s claim that the passenger compartment is "in fact generally, even if not inevitably," within the suspect's immediate control (cite omitted). By the United States' own admission, however, "the practice of restraining an arrestee on the scene before searching a car that he just occupied is so prevalent that holding that *Belton* does not apply in that setting would . . . 'largely render *Belton* a dead letter.' "(cites omitted). Reported cases involving this precise factual scenario—a motorist handcuffed and secured in the back of a squad car when the search takes place—are legion (cites omitted). Some courts uphold such searches even when the squad car carrying the handcuffed arrestee has already left the scene (cite omitted).

The popularity of the practice is not hard to fathom. If *Belton* entitles an officer to search a vehicle upon arresting the driver despite having taken measures that eliminate any danger, what rational officer would not take those measures? Cf. Moskovitz, A Rule in Search of a Reason: An Empirical Reexamination of *Chimel* and *Belton*, 2002 Wis. L. Rev. 657, 665–666 (citing police training materials). If it was ever true that the passenger compartment is "in fact generally, even if not inevitably," within the arrestee's immediate control at the time of the search, (cite omitted), it certainly is not true today. As one judge has put it: "In our search for clarity, we have now abandoned our constitutional moorings and floated to a place where the law approves of purely exploratory searches of vehicles during which officers with no definite objective or reason for the search are allowed to rummage around in a car to see what they might find." *McLaughlin* supra, at 894 (Trott, J., concurring). I agree entirely with that assessment.

II

If *Belton* searches are justifiable, it is not because the arrestee might grab a weapon or evidentiary item from his car, but simply because the car might contain evidence relevant to the crime for which he was arrested. This more general sort of evidence-gathering search is not without antecedent. For example, in *United States* v. *Rabinowitz,* 339 U.S. 56, 70 S. Ct. 430 (1950), we upheld a search of the suspect's place of business after he was arrested there. We did not restrict the officers' search authority to "the area into which [the] arrestee might reach in order to grab a weapon or evidentiary item," *Chimel*, (cite omitted), and we did not justify the search as a means to prevent concealment or destruction of evidence. Rather, we relied on a more general interest in gathering evidence relevant to the crime for which the suspect had been arrested (cite omitted).

Numerous earlier authorities support this approach, referring to the general interest in gathering evidence related to the crime of arrest with no mention of the more specific interest in preventing its concealment or destruction (cites omitted).... Only in the years leading up to *Chimel* did we start consistently referring to the narrower interest in frustrating concealment or destruction of evidence (cite omitted).

There is nothing irrational about broader police authority to search for evidence when and where the perpetrator of a crime is lawfully arrested. The fact of prior lawful arrest distinguishes the arrestee from society at large, and distinguishes a search for evidence of *his* crime from general rummaging. Moreover, it is not illogical to assume that evidence of a crime is most likely to be found where the suspect was apprehended.

Nevertheless, *Chimel*'s narrower focus on concealment or destruction of evidence also has historical support (cites omitted) ...

In short, both *Rabinowitz* and *Chimel* are plausible accounts of what the Constitution requires, and neither is so persuasive as to justify departing from settled law. But if we are going to continue to allow *Belton* searches on *stare decisis* grounds, we should at least be honest about why we are doing so. *Belton* cannot reasonably be explained as a mere application of *Chimel*. Rather, it is a return to the broader sort of search incident to arrest that we allowed before *Chimel*—limited, of course, to searches of motor vehicles, a category of "effects" which give rise to a reduced expectation of privacy, see *Wyoming* v. *Houghton,* 526 U.S. 295, 303, 119 S. Ct. 1297 (1999), and heightened law enforcement needs, see 526 U.S. at 304, 119 S. Ct. 1297; *Rabinowitz,* 339 U.S., at 73, 70 S. Ct. 430 (Frankfurter, J., dissenting).

Recasting *Belton* in these terms would have at least one important practical consequence. In *United States* v. *Robinson,* (cite omitted), we held that authority to search an arrestee's person does not depend on the actual presence of one of *Chimel*'s two rationales in the particular case; rather, the fact of arrest alone justifies the search. That holding stands in contrast to *Rabinowitz,* where we did not treat the fact of arrest alone as sufficient, but upheld the search only after noting that it was "not general or exploratory for whatever might be turned up" but reflected a reasonable belief that evidence would be found (cites omitted) The two different rules make sense: When officer safety or imminent evidence concealment or destruction is at issue, officers should not have to make fine judgments in the heat of the moment. But in the context of a general evidence-gathering search, the state interests that might justify any overbreadth are far less compelling. A motorist may be arrested for a wide variety of offenses; in many cases, there is no reasonable basis to believe relevant evidence might be found in the car. See *Atwater* v. *Lago Vista,* (cite omitted). I would therefore limit *Belton* searches to cases where it is reasonable to believe evidence relevant to the crime of arrest might be found in the vehicle.

In this case, as in *Belton*, petitioner was lawfully arrested for a drug offense. It was reasonable for Officer Nichols to believe that further contraband or similar evidence relevant to the crime for which he had been arrested might be found in the vehicle from which he had just alighted and which was still within his vicinity at the time of arrest. I would affirm the decision below on that ground.

■ DISSENT: Justice Stevens, with whom Justice Souter joins, dissenting.

Prior to our decision in *New York* v. *Belton,* (cite omitted), there was a widespread conflict among both federal and state courts over the question "whether, in the course of a search incident to the lawful custodial arrest of the occupants of an automobile, police may search inside the automobile after the arrestees are no longer in it" (cite omitted). In answering that question, the Court expanded the authority of the police in two important respects. It allowed the police to conduct a broader search than our decision in *Chimel* v. *California*, (cite omitted), would have permitted, and it authorized them to open closed containers that might be found in the vehicle's passenger compartment.

The bright-line rule crafted in *Belton* is not needed for cases in which the arrestee is first accosted when he is a pedestrian, because *Chimel* itself provides all the guidance that is necessary. The only genuine justification for extending *Belton* to cover such circumstances is the interest in uncovering potentially valuable evidence. In my opinion, that goal must give way to the citizen's constitutionally protected interest in privacy when there is already in place a well-defined rule limiting the permissible scope of a search of an arrested pedestrian. The *Chimel* rule should provide the same protection to a "recent occupant" of a vehicle as to a recent occupant of a house.

Unwilling to confine the *Belton* rule to the narrow class of cases it was designed to address, the Court extends *Belton*'s reach without supplying any guidance for the future application of its swollen rule. We are told that officers may search a vehicle incident to arrest "so long as [the] arrestee is the sort of 'recent occupant' of a vehicle such as petitioner was here" (cite omitted). But we are not told how recent is recent, or how close is close, perhaps because in this case "the record is not clear" (cite omitted). As the Court cautioned in *Belton* itself, "when a person cannot know how a court will apply a settled principle to a recurring factual situation, that person cannot know the scope of his constitutional protection, nor can a policeman know the scope of his authority" (cite omitted). Without some limiting principle, I fear that today's decision will contribute to "a massive broadening of the automobile exception," *Robbins*, 453 U.S., at 452, 101 S. Ct. 2841 (Stevens, J., dissenting), when officers have probable cause to arrest an individual but not to search his car.

Accordingly, I respectfully dissent.

H. MOTOR VEHICLE SEARCHES

Add to note (2)(c) on page 476:

Note that many states have laws that create a presumption that if contraband is found within a car, all the occupants are presumed to possess the contraband unless there is other evidence to the contrary. See e.g. Maryland v. Pringle, ___ U.S. ___, 124 S.Ct. 795 (2003). Thus there may be some overlap between a motor vehicle search and a search incident to the arrest of an occupant within a vehicle.

K. STOP-AND-FRISK AND OTHER LIMITED INVESTIGATIVE DETENTIONS

Add at end of note 2 on page 512:

In *Florida v. J.L.,* 529 U.S. 266, 120 S.Ct. 1375 (2000) the police frisked a defendant after receiving an anonymous tip that a young black male standing at a particular bus stop and wearing a plaid shirt was carrying a gun. They saw no firearm or unusual movements prior to their action. The Court held that this was insufficient to justify the frisk and thus the gun that was recovered from the defendant's pocket was the fruit of an illegal stop and frisk. The Court refrained from converting *Terry* into a "firearms exception" to the Fourth Amendment.

Add after note E on page 522:

May police require that a suspect provide a name? Identification? A video of the events that form the basis of the case that follows is available on the defendant's website at http://papersplease.org/hiibel/index2.html.

Hiibel v. Sixth Judicial District Court of Nevada, Humboldt County, et. al.

___ U.S. ___, 124 S.Ct. 2451 (June 21, 2004).

■ JUSTICE KENNEDY delivered the opinion of the Court.

The petitioner was arrested and convicted for refusing to identify himself during a stop allowed by *Terry v. Ohio*, 392 U.S. 1, 88 S. Ct.1868 (1968). He challenges his conviction under the Fourth and Fifth Amendments to the United States Constitution, applicable to the States through the Fourteenth Amendment.

I

The sheriff's department in Humboldt County, Nevada, received an afternoon telephone call reporting an assault. The caller reported seeing a man a woman in a red and silver GMC truck on Grass Valley Road. Deputy Sheriff Lee Dove was dispatched to investigate. When the officer arrived at the scene, he found the truck parked on the side of the road. A man was standing by the truck, and a young woman was sitting inside it. The officer observed skid marks in the gravel behind the vehicle, leading him to believe it had come to a sudden stop.

The officer approached the man and explained that he was investigating a report of a fight. The man appeared to be intoxicated. The officer asked him if he had "any identification on [him]," which we understand as a request to produce a driver's license or some other form of written identification. The man refused and asked why the officer wanted to see identification. The officer responded that he was conducting an investigation and needed to see some identification. The unidentified man became agitated and insisted he had done nothing wrong. The officer explained that he wanted to find out who the man was and what he was doing there. After continued refusals to comply with the officer's request for identification, the man began to taunt the officer by placing his hands behind his back and telling the officer to arrest him and take him to jail. This routine kept up for several minutes: the officer asked for identification 11 times and was refused each time. After warning the man that he would be arrested is he continued to refuse to comply, the officer placed him under arrest.

We now know that the man arrested on Grass Valley Road is Larry Dudley Hiibel. Hiibel was charged with "willfully resisting, delaying, or obstructing a public officer in discharging or attempting to discharge any legal duty of his office" in violation of Nev. Rev. Stat. (NRS) § 199.280 (2003). The government reasoned that Hiibel had obstructed the officer in carrying out his duties under § 171.123, a Nevada statute that defines the legal rights and duties of a police officer in the context of an investigative stop. Section 171.123 provides in relevant part:

> 1. Any peace officer may detain any person whom the officer encounters under circumstances which reasonably indicate that the person has committed, is committing or is about to commit a crime.
>
> . . .
>
> 3. The officer may detain the person pursuant to this section only to ascertain his identity and the suspicious circumstances surrounding his presence aboard. Any person so detained shall identify himself, but may not be compelled to answer any other inquiry of any peace officer.

Hiibel was tried in the Justice Court of Union Township. The court agreed that Hiibel's refusal to identify himself as required by § 171.123 "obstructed and delayed Dove as a public officer in attempting to discharge his duty" in violation of § 199.280.... Hiibel was convicted and fined $250. The Sixth Judicial District Court affirmed, rejecting Hiibel's argument that the application of § 171.123 to his case violated the Fourth and Fifth Amendments. On review the Supreme Court of Nevada rejected the Fourth Amendment challenge in a divided opinion. Hiibel petitioned for rehearing, seeking explicit resolution of his Fifth Amendment challenge. The petition was denied without opinion. We granted certiorari.

II

NRS § 171.123(3) is an enactment sometimes referred to as a "stop and identify" statute (cites omitted).

Stop and identify statutes often combine elements of traditional vagrancy laws with provisions intended to regulate police behavior in the course of investigatory stops. The statutes vary from State to State, but all permit an officer to ask or require a suspect to disclose his identity.... In some States, a suspect's refusal to identify himself is a misdemeanor offense or civil violation; in others, it is a factor to be considered in whether the suspect has violated loitering laws. In other States, a suspect may decline to identify himself without penalty.

Stop and identify statutes have their root in early English vagrancy laws that required suspected vagrants to face arrest unless they gave a "a good Account of themselves," (cite omitted) a power that itself reflected common-law rights of private persons to "arrest any suspicious night-walker, and detain him till he gave a good account of himself ...." (cite omitted) In recent decades, the Court has found constitutional infirmity in traditional vagrancy laws. In *Papachristou v. Jacksonville*, 405 U.S. 156, 92 S.Ct. 839 (1972), the Court held that a traditional vagrancy law was void for vagueness. Its broad scope and imprecise terms denied proper notice to potential offenders and permitted police officers to exercise unfettered discretion in the enforcement of the law.

The Court has recognized similar constitutional limitations on the scope and operation of stop and identify statutes. In Brown v. Texas, 443 U.S. 47, 99 S.Ct. 2637 (1979), the Court invalidated a conviction for violating a Texas stop and identify statute on Fourth Amendment grounds. The Court ruled that the initial stop was not based on specific, objective facts establishing reasonable suspicion to believe the suspect was involved in criminal activity (cite omitted). Absent that factual basis for detaining the defendant, the Court held, the risk of "arbitrary and abusive police practices" was too great and the stop was impermissible(cite omitted). Four Terms later, the Court invalidated a modified stop and identify statute of vagueness grounds. See *Kolender v. Lawson*, 461 U.S. 352 , 103 S.Ct. 1855 (1983). The California law in *Kolender* required a suspect to give an officer " 'credible and reliable' " identification when asked to identify himself. The Court held that the statute was void because it provided no standard for determining what a suspect must do to comply with it, resulting in " 'virtually unrestrained power to arrest and charge persons with a violation' " (cite omitted).

The present case begins where our prior cases left off. Here there is no question that the initial stop was based on reasonable suspicion, satisfying the Fourth Amendment requirements noted in *Brown*. Further, the petitioner has not alleged that the statute is unconstitutionally vague, as in *Kolender*. Here the Nevada statute is narrower and more precise. The statute in Kolender has been interpreted to require a suspect to give the officer "credible and reliable" identification. In contrast, the Nevada Supreme Court has interpreted NRS § 171.123(3) to require only that a suspect disclose his name.... As we understand it, the statute does not require a suspect to give the officer a driver's license or any other document. Provided that the suspect either states his name or communicates it to officer by other means–a choice, we assume, that the suspect may make–the statute is satisfied and no violation occurs (cite omitted).

III

Hiibel argues that his conviction cannot stand because the officer's conduct violated his Fourth Amendment rights. We disagree.

Asking questions is an essential part of police investigations. In the ordinary course a police officer is free to ask a person for identification without implicating the Fourth Amendment. "Interrogation relating to one's identity or a request for identification by the police does not by itself constitute a Fourth Amendment seizure." *INS v. Delgado*, 466 U.S. 210, 104 S.Ct. 1758 (1984). Beginning with *Terry v. Ohio* (cite omitted) (1968), the Court has recognized that a law enforcement officer's reasonable suspicion that a person may be involved in criminal activity permits the officer to stop the person for a brief time and take additional steps to investigate further, *Delgado*, (cite omitted), *United States v. Brignoni–Ponce*, 422 U.S. 873, 95 S.Ct. 2574 (1975). To ensure that the resulting seizure is constitutionally reasonable, a *Terry* stop must be limited. The officer's action must be " 'justified at its inception, and.... reasonably related in scope to the circumstances which justified the interference in the first place.' " *United States v. Sharpe*, 470 U.S. 675, 105 S. Ct. 1568 (1985)(quoting *Terry*, (cite omitted)). For example, the seizure cannot continue for an excessive period of time, see *United States* v. *Place,* 462 U.S. 696, 709, 103 S. Ct. 2637 (1983), or resemble a traditional arrest, see *Dunaway* v. *New York,* 442 U.S. 200, 212, 99 S. Ct. 2248 (1979).

Our decisions make clear that questions concerning a suspect's identity are a routine and accepted part of many *Terry* stops. See *United States v. Hensley,* 469 U.S. 221, 105 S.Ct. 675 (1985) ("The ability to briefly stop [a suspect], ask questions, or check identification in the absence of probable cause promotes the strong government interest in solving crimes and bringing offenders to justice"); *Hayes v. Florida*, 470 U.S. 811, 816, 105 S. Ct. 1643 (1985) ("If there are articulable facts supporting a reasonable suspicion that a person has committed a criminal offense, that person may be stopped in order to identify him, to question him briefly, or to detain him briefly while attempting to obtain additional information"); *Adams v. Williams,* 407 U.S. 143, 92 S.Ct. 1921 (1972) ("A brief stop of a suspicious individual, in order to determine his ability or to maintain the status quo momentarily while obtaining more information, may be most reasonable in light of the facts known to the officer at the time").

Obtaining a suspect's name in the course of a *Terry* stops serves important government interests. Knowledge of identity may inform an officer that a suspect is wanted for another offense, or has a record of violence or mental disorder. On the other hand, knowing identity may help clear a suspect and allow the police to concentrate their efforts elsewhere. Identity may prove particularly important in cases such as this, where the police are investigating what appears to be a domestic assault. Officers called to investigate domestic disputes need to know whom they are dealing with in order to assess the situation, the threat to their own safety, and possible danger to the potential victim.

Although it is well established that an officer may ask a suspect to identify himself in the course of a *Terry* stop, it has been an open question whether the suspect can be arrested and prosecuted for refusal to answer. See Brown (cite omitted) Petitioner draws our attention to statements in prior opinions that, according to him, answer the question in his favor. In *Terry*, Justice White stated in a concurring opinion that a person detained in an investigative stop can be questioned but is "not obliged to answer, answers may not be compelled, and refusal to answer furnishes no basis for an arrest." 392 U.S. 1, at 34, 88 S.Ct. 1868 . . The Court cited this opinion in dicta in *Berkemer v. McCarty*, 468 U.S. 420, 104 S.Ct. 3138 (1984), a decision holding that a routine traffic stop is not a custodial stop requiring the protections of *Miranda v. Arizona*, (cite omitted). In the course of explaining why *Terry* stops have not been subject to *Miranda*, the Court suggested reasons why *Terry* stops have a "nonthreatening character," among them the fact that a suspect detained during a *Terry* stop "is not obliged to respond" to questions (cite omitted). According to petitioner, these statements establish a right to refuse to answer questions during a *Terry* stop.

We do not read these statements as controlling. The passages recognize that the Fourth Amendment does not impose obligations on the citizen but instead provides rights against the government. As a result, the Fourth Amendment itself cannot require a suspect to answer questions. This case concerns a different issue, however. Here, the source of the legal obligation arises from Nevada state law, not the Fourth Amendment. Further, the statutory obligation does not go beyond answering an officer's request to disclose a name. See NRS § 171.123(3)("Any person so detained shall identify himself, but may not be compelled to answer any other inquiry of any peace officer"). As a result, we cannot view the dicta in *Berkemer* of Justice White's concurrence in *Terry* as answering the question whether a State can compel a suspect to disclose his name during a *Terry* stop.

The principles of *Terry* permits a State to require a suspect to disclose his name in the course of a *Terry* stop. The reasonableness of a seizure under the Fourth Amendment is determined "by balancing its intrusion on the individual's Fourth Amendment interests against its promotion of legitimate government interest." *Delaware v. Prouse,* 440 U.S. 648, 99 S.Ct. 1391 (1979). The Nevada statute satisfies that standard. The request for identity has an immediate relation to the purpose, rationale, and practical demands of a *Terry* stop. The threat of criminal sanction helps ensure that the request for identity does not become a legal nullity. On the other hand, the Nevada statute does not alter the nature of the stop itself: it does not change its duration. A state law requiring a suspect to disclose his name in the course of a valid *Terry* stop is consistent with Fourth Amendment prohibitions against unreasonable searches and seizures.

Petitioner argues that the Nevada statute circumvents the probable cause requirement, in effect allowing an officer to arrest a person for being suspicious. According to petitioner, this creates a risk of arbitrary police conduct that the Fourth Amendment does not permit. Brief for Petitioner 28–33. These are familiar concerns; they were central to the opinion in *Papachristou*, and also to the decisions limiting the operation of stop and identify statutes in *Kolender* and *Brown*. Petitioner's concerns are met by the requirement that a *Terry* stop must be justified at its inception and "reasonably related in scope to the circumstances which justified" the initial stop. 392 U.S.1, at 20. Under these principles, an officer may not arrest a suspect for failure to identify himself if the request for identification is not reasonably related to the circumstances justifying the stop. The

Court noted a similar limitation in *Hayes*, where it suggested that *Terry* may permit an officer to determine a suspect's identity by compelling the suspect to submit to fingerprinting only if there is "reasonable basis for believing that fingerprinting will establish or negate the suspect's connection with that crime"(cite omitted). It is clear in this case that the request for identification was "reasonably related in scope to the circumstances which justified" the stop. *Terry* (cite omitted). The officer's request was a commonsense inquiry, not an effort to obtain an arrest for failure to identify after a Terry stop yielded insufficient evidence. The stop, the request, and the State's requirement of a response did not contravene the guarantees of the Fourth Amendment.

IV

Petitioner further contends that his conviction violates the Fifth Amendment's prohibition on compelled self-incrimination. The Fifth Amendment states that."no person ... shall be compelled in any criminal case to be a witness against himself." To qualify for the Fifth Amendment privilege, a communication must be testimonial, incriminating, and compelled. See *United States* v. *Hubbell,* (cite omitted).

Respondents urge us to hold that the statements NRS § 171.123(3) requires are nontestimonial, and so outside the Clause's scope. We decline to resolve the case on that basis. "To be testimonial, an accused's communication must itself, explicitly or implicitly, relate a factual assertion or disclose information." *Doe v. United States*, 487 U.S. 201, 108 S. Ct. 2341 (1988). Stating one's name may qualify as an assertion of fact relating to identity. Production of identity documents might meet the definition as well. As we noted in *Hubbell*, acts of production may yield testimony establishing "the existence, authenticity, and custody of items [the police seek]" (cite omitted). Even if these required actions are testimonial, however, petitioner's challenge must fail because in his case disclosure of his name presented no reasonable danger of incrimination.

The Fifth Amendment prohibits only compelled testimony that is incriminating....

In this case petitioner's refusal to disclose his name was not based on any articulated real and appreciable fear that his name would be used to incriminate him, or that it "would furnish a link in the chain of evidence needed to prosecute" him. Hoffman v. United States, 341 U.S. 479, 71 S.Ct. 814 (1951). As best we can tell, petitioner refused to identify himself only because he thought his name was none of the officer's business. Even today, petitioner does not explain how the disclosure of his name could have been used against him in a criminal case. While we recognize petitioner's strong belief that he should not have to disclose his identity, the Fifth Amendment does not override the Nevada Legislature's judgment to the contrary absent a reasonable belief that the disclosure would tend to incriminate him.

The narrow scope of the disclosure requirement is also important. One's identity is, by definition, unique; yet it is, in another sense, a universal characteristic. Answering a request to disclose a name is likely to be so insignificant in the scheme of things as to be incriminating only in unusual circumstances (cites omitted).... Even witnesses who plan to invoke the Fifth Amendment privilege answer when their names are called to take the stand. Still, a case may arise where there is a substantial allegation that furnishing identity at the time of a stop would have given the police a link in the chain of evidence needed to convict the individual of a separate offense. In that case, the court can then consider whether the privilege applies, and, if the Fifth Amendment has been violated, what remedy must follow. We need not resolve those questions here.

The judgment of the Nevada Supreme Court is

Affirmed.

■ JUSTICE STEVENS, dissenting.

The Nevada law at issue in this case imposes a narrow duty to speak upon a specific class of individuals. The class includes only those persons detained by a police officer "under circumstances which reasonably indicate that the person has committed, is committing or is about to commit a crime"–persons who are, in other words, targets of a criminal investigation. The statute therefore is directed not "at the public at large," but rather "at a highly selective group inherently suspect of criminal activities"(cite omitted).

Under the Nevada law, a member of the targeted class "may not be compelled to answer" any inquiry except a command that he "identify himself." Refusal to identify oneself upon request is punishable as a crime. Presumably the statute does not require the detainee to answer any other question because the Nevada Legislature realized that the Fifth Amendment prohibits compelling the target of a criminal investigation to make any other statement. In my judgment, the broad constitutional right to remain silent, which derives from the Fifth Amendment's guarantee that "no person ... shall be compelled in any criminal case to be a witness against himself." U.S. Const. Amdt. 5, is not as circumscribed as the Court suggests, and does not admit even of the narrow exception defined by the Nevada statute.

"There can be no doubt that the Fifth Amendment privilege is available outside of criminal court proceedings and serves to protect persons in all settings in which their freedom of action is curtailed in any significant way from being compelled to incriminate themselves." *Miranda v. Arizona*, (cite omitted). It is a "settled principle" that "the police have the right to request citizens to answer voluntarily questions concerning unsolved crimes," but "they have no right to compel them to answer." *Davis v. Mississippi*, 394 U.S. 721, 89 S.Ct. 1394 (1969). The protections of the Fifth Amendment are directed squarely toward those who are the focus of the government's investigative and prosecutorial powers. In a criminal trial, the indicted defendant has an unqualified right to refuse to testify and not be punished for invoking that right (cites omitted). The unindicted target of a grand jury investigation enjoys the same constitutional protection even if he has been served with a subpoena (cite omitted). So does an arrested suspect during custodial interrogation in a police station (cite omitted).

There is no reason why the subject of police interrogation based on mere suspicion, rather than probable cause, should have any lesser protection. Indeed, we have said that the Fifth Amendment's protections apply with equal force in the context of *Terry* stops (cite omitted), where an officer's inquiry "must be reasonably related in scope to the justification for [the stop's] initiation." *Berkemer v. McCarty*, 468 U.S. 420, 439, 104 S.Ct. 3138 (1984) [some internal quotation marks omitted in original]. "Typically this means that the officer may ask the detainee a moderate number of questions to determine his identity and to try to obtain information confirming or dispelling the officer's suspicions. But the detainee is not obliged to respond." See also *Terry*, (cite omitted) (White, J., concurring) ("Of course, the person stopped is not obliged to answer, answers may not be compelled, and refusal to answer furnishes no basis for arrest, although it may alert the officer to te need for continued observation"). Given our statements to the effect that citizens are not required respond to police officers' questions during a Terry stop, it is no surprise that petitioner assumed, as have we, that he had a right not to disclose his identity.

The Court correctly observes that a communication does not enjoy the Fifth Amendment privilege unless it is testimonial. Although the Court declines to resolve this question, I think it clear that this case concerns a testimonial communication. Recognizing that whether a communication is testimonial is sometimes a "difficult question," *Doe* v. *United States*, (cite omitted), we have stated generally that "it is the 'extortion of information from the accused,' the attempt to force him 'to disclose the contents of his own mind,' that implicates the Self–Incrimination Clause," (cite with citations omitted). While "the vast majority of verbal statements thus will be testimonial and, to that extent at least, will fall within the privilege," (cite omitted), certain acts and physical evidence fall outside the privilege.[1] In all instances, we have afforded Fifth Amendment protection if the disclosure in question was being admitted because of its content rather than some other aspect of the communication.

Considered in light of these precedents, the compelled statement at issue in this case is clearly testimonial. It is significant that the communication must be made in response to a question posed by a police officer. Surely police questioning during a *Terry* stop qualifies as an interrogation, and it follows that response to such questions are testimonial in nature. As we recently explained, albeit in the different context of the Sixth Amendment's Confrontation Clause, "whatever else the term ['testimonial'] covers, it applies at a minimum . . . to police interrogations." *Crawford* v. *Washington,* 541 U.S. ___, ___, 124 S. Ct. 1354 (2004). Surely police questioning during a *Terry* stop qualifies as an interrogation, and it follows that responses to such questions are testimonial in nature.

Rather than determining whether the communication at issue is testimonial, the Court instead concludes that the State can compel the disclosure of one's identity because it is not "incriminating." But our cases have afforded Fifth Amendment protection to statements that are "incriminating" in a much broader sense than the Court suggests. It has "long been

1. A suspect may be made, for example, to provide a blood sample, *Schmerber* v. *California,* 384 U.S. 757, 765, 86 S. Ct. 1826 (1966), a voice exemplar, *United States* v. *Dionisio,* 410 U.S. 1, 7, 93 S. Ct. 764 (1973), or a handwriting sample, *Gilbert* v. *California,* 388 U.S. 263, 266–267, 87 S. Ct. 1951 (1967).

settled that [the Fifth Amendment's] protection encompasses compelled statements that lead to the discovery of incriminating evidence even though the statements themselves are not incriminating and are not introduced into evidence'' (cite omitted). . . . Thus, ''compelled testimony that communicates information that may 'lead to incriminating evidence' is privileged even if the information itself is not inculpatory'' (cites omitted).

Given a proper understanding of the category of ''incriminating'' communications that fall within the Fifth Amendment privilege, it is clear that the disclosure of petitioner's identity is protected. The Court reasons that we should not assume that the disclosure of petitioner's name would be used to incriminate him or that it would furnish a link in a chain of evidence needed to prosecute him. But why else would an officer ask for it? And why else would the Nevada Legislature require its disclosure only when circumstances ''reasonably indicate that the person has committed, is committing or is about to commit a crime''? If the Court is correct, then petitioner's refusal to cooperate did not impede the police investigation. Indeed, if we accept the predicate for the Court's holding, the statute requires nothing more than a useless invasion of privacy. I think that, on the contrary, the Nevada Legislature intended to provide its police officers with a useful law enforcement tool, and that the very existence of the statute demonstrates the value of the information it demands.

A person's identity obviously bears informational and incriminating worth, ''even if the [name] itself is not inculpatory'' (cite omitted). A name can provide the key to a broad array of information about the person, particularly in the hands of a police officer with access to a range of law enforcement databases. And that information, in turn, can be tremendously useful in a criminal prosecution. It is therefore quite wrong to suggest that a person's identity provides a link in the chain to incriminating evidence ''only in unusual circumstances.''

The officer in the case told petitioner, in the Court's words, that ''he was conducting an investigation and needed to see some identification.'' As the target of that investigation, petitioner, in my view, acted well within his rights when he opted to stand mute. According, I respectfully dissent.

■ JUSTICE BREYER, with whom JUSTICE SOUTER and JUSTICE GINSBURG join, dissenting.

Notwithstanding the vagrancy statutes to which the majority refers, this Court's Fourth Amendment precedents make clear that police may conduct a *Terry* stop only within circumscribed limits. And one of those limits invalidates laws that compel responses to police questioning.

In *Terry v. Ohio*, (cite omitted), the Court considered whether police, in the absence of probable cause, can stop, questions, or frisk an individual at all. . . . At the same time, it recognized that in certain circumstances, public safety might require a limited ''seizure,'' or stop, of an individual against his will. The Court consequently set forth conditions circumscribing when and how the police might conduct a *Terry* stop. They include what has become known as the ''reasonable suspicion'' standard (cite omitted). Justice White, in a separate concurring opinion, set forth further conditions. Justice White wrote: ''Of course, the person stopped is not obliged to answer, answer may not be compelled, and refusal to answer furnishes no basis for an arrest, although it may alert the officer to the need for continued observation." (cite omitted).

About 10 years later, the Court, in *Brown v. Texas* (cite omitted) held that police lacked "any reasonable suspicion" to detain the particular petitioner and require him to identify himself. The Court noted that the trial judge had asked the following: "I'm sure [officers conducting a *Terry* stop] should ask everything they possibly could find out. *What I'm asking is what's the State's interest in putting a man in jail because he doesn't want to answer....*" (cite omitted)(emphasis in the original).... The Court referred to Justice White's *Terry* concurrence (cite omitted). 443 U.S. 47, at 53, n. 3. And it said that it "need not decide" the matter.

Then, five years later, the Court wrote that an "officer may ask the [*Terry*] detainee a moderate number of questions to determine his identity and to try to obtain information confirming or dispelling the officer's suspicions. *But the detainee is not obliged to respond.*" *Berkemer v. McCarty*, (cite omitted) (emphasis added in original). See also *Kolender v. Lawson*, (cite omitted) (Brennan, J., concurring) (Terry suspect "must be free to ... decline to answer the questions put to him); *Illinois v. Wardlow*, (cite omitted)('stating that allowing officers to stop and question a fleeing person' is quite consistent with the individual's right to go about his business or to stay put and remain silent in the fact of police questioning").

This lengthy history–of concurring opinions, of references, and of clear explicit statements–means that the Court's statement in *Berkemer,* while technically dicta, is the kind of strong dicta that the legal community typically takes as a statement of the law. And that law has remained undisturbed for more than 20 years.

There is no good reason now to reject this generation-old statement of the law. There are sound reasons rooted in Fifth Amendment considerations for adhering to this Fourth Amendment legal condition circumscribing police authority to stop an individual against his will. Administrative considerations also militate against change. Can a State, in addition to requiring a stopped individual to answer "What's your name?" also require an answer to "What's your license number?" or "Where do you live?" Can a police officer, who must know how to make a Terry stop, keep track of the constitutional answers? After all, answers to any of these questions may, or may not, incriminate, depending upon the circumstances.

Indeed, as the majority points out, a name itself–even if it not "Killer Bill" or "Rough 'em up Harry"–will sometimes provide the police with a link in the chain of evidence needed to convict the individual of a separate offense. The majority reserves judgment about whether compulsion is permissible in such instances. How then is a police officer in the midst of a *Terry* stop to distinguish between the majority's ordinary case and this special case where the majority reserves judgment?

The majority presents no evidence that the rule enunciated by Justice White and then by the *Berkemer* Court, which for nearly a generation has set forth a settled *Terry* stop condition, has significantly interfered with law enforcement. Nor has the majority presented any other convincing justification for change. I would not begin to erode a clear rule with special exceptions.

I consequently dissent.

L. ADMINISTRATIVE AND "SPECIAL NEEDS" SEARCHES

Add before the first full paragraph on page 545:

1.b. *Drug Testing of Students*

Add at the end of note 3 on page 547:

The Court has approved highway checkpoints vehicle roadblocks established to ask motorists if they had information about a crime that had occurred earlier at the location.

Illinois v. Lidster

___ U.S. ___, 124 S.Ct. 885 (January 13, 2004).

■ JUDGES: BREYER, J., delivered the opinion of the Court, in which REHNQUIST, C. J., and O'CONNOR, SCALIA, KENNEDY, and THOMAS, JJ., joined, and in which STEVENS, SOUTER, and GINSBURG, JJ., joined as to Parts I and II. STEVENS, J., filed an opinion concurring in part and dissenting in part, in which SOUTER and GINSBURG, JJ., joined.

■ JUSTICE BREYER delivered the opinion of the Court.

This Fourth Amendment case focuses upon a highway checkpoint where police stopped motorists to ask them for information about a recent hit-and-run accident. We hold that the police stops were reasonable, hence, constitutional.

I

The relevant background is as follows: On Saturday, August 23, 1997, just after midnight, an unknown motorist traveling eastbound on a highway in Lombard, Illinois, struck and killed a 70–year-old bicyclist. The motorist drove off without identifying himself. About one week later at about the same time of night and at about the same place, local police set up a highway checkpoint designed to obtain more information about the accident from the motoring public.

Police cars with flashing lights partially blocked the eastbound lanes of the highway. The blockage forced traffic to slow down, leading to lines of up to 15 cars in each lane. As each vehicle drew up to the checkpoint, an officer would stop it for 10 to 15 seconds, ask the occupants whether they had seen anything happen there the previous weekend, and hand each driver a flyer. The flyer said "ALERT ... FATAL HIT & RUN ACCIDENT" and requested "assistance in identifying the vehicle and driver in this accident which killed a 70 year old bicyclist."

Robert Lidster, the respondent, drove a minivan toward the checkpoint. As he approached the checkpoint, his van swerved, nearly hitting one of the officers. The officer smelled alcohol on Lidster's breath. He directed

Lidster to a side street where another officer administered a sobriety test and then arrested Lidster. Lidster was tried and convicted in Illinois state court of driving under the influence of alcohol.

Lidster challenged the lawfulness of his arrest and conviction on the ground that the government had obtained much of the relevant evidence through use of a checkpoint stop that violated the Fourth Amendment. The trial court rejected that challenge. But an Illinois appellate court reached the opposite conclusion (cite omitted). The Illinois Supreme Court agreed with the appellate court. It held (by a vote of 4 to 3) that our decision in *Indianapolis* v. *Edmond,* 531 U.S. 32, 121 S. Ct. 447 (2000), required it to find the stop unconstitutional (cite omitted).

Because lower courts have reached different conclusions about this matter, we granted certiorari (cite omitted).

II

The Illinois Supreme Court basically held that our decision in *Edmond* governs the outcome of this case. We do not agree. *Edmond* involved a checkpoint at which police stopped vehicles to look for evidence of drug crimes committed by occupants of those vehicles. After stopping a vehicle at the checkpoint, police would examine (from outside the vehicle) the vehicle's interior; they would walk a drug-sniffing dog around the exterior; and, if they found sufficient evidence of drug (or other) crimes, they would arrest the vehicle's occupants. 531 U.S., at 35, 121 S. Ct. 447. We found that police had set up this checkpoint primarily for general "crime control" purposes, *i.e.*, "to detect evidence of ordinary criminal wrongdoing" (cite omitted). We noted that the stop was made without individualized suspicion. And we held that the Fourth Amendment forbids such a stop, in the absence of special circumstances (cite omitted).

The checkpoint stop here differs significantly from that in *Edmond.* The stop's primary law enforcement purpose was *not* to determine whether a vehicle's occupants were committing a crime, but to ask vehicle occupants, as members of the public, for their help in providing information about a crime in all likelihood committed by others. The police expected the information elicited to help them apprehend, not the vehicle's occupants, but other individuals.

Edmond's language, as well as its context, makes clear that the constitutionality of this latter, information-seeking kind of stop was not then before the Court. *Edmond* refers to the subject matter of its holding as "stops justified only by the generalized and ever-present possibility that interrogation and inspection may reveal that *any given motorist has committed some crime.*" (emphasis added). We concede that *Edmond* describes the law enforcement objective there in question as a "general interest in crime control," but it specifies that the phrase "general interest in crime control" does not refer to every "law enforcement" objective (cite omitted). We must read this and related general language in *Edmond* as we often read general language in judicial opinions—as referring in context to circumstances similar to the circumstances then before the Court and not referring to quite different circumstances that the Court was not then considering.

Neither do we believe, *Edmond* aside, that the Fourth Amendment would have us apply an *Edmond*-type rule of automatic unconstitutionality to brief, information-seeking highway stops of the kind now before us. For one thing, the fact that such stops normally lack individualized suspicion cannot by itself determine the constitutional outcome. As in *Edmond,* the stop here at issue involves a motorist. The Fourth Amendment does not treat a motorist's car as his castle (cites omitted). And special law enforcement concerns will sometimes justify highway stops without individualized suspicion. See *Michigan Dept. of State Police* v. *Sitz*, 496 U.S. 444, 110 S. Ct. 2481 (1990) (sobriety checkpoint); *Martinez-Fuerte*, *supra* (Border Patrol checkpoint). Moreover, unlike *Edmond*, the context here (seeking information from the public) is one in which, by definition, the concept of individualized suspicion has little role to play. Like certain other forms of police activity, say, crowd control or public safety, an information-seeking stop is not the kind of event that involves suspicion, or lack of suspicion, of the relevant individual.

For another thing, information-seeking highway stops are less likely to provoke anxiety or to prove intrusive. The stops are likely brief. The police are not likely to ask questions designed to elicit self-incriminating information. And citizens will often react positively when police simply ask for their help as "responsible citizen[s]" to "give whatever information they may have to aid in law enforcement." *Miranda* v. *Arizona*, (cite omitted).

Further, the law ordinarily permits police to seek the voluntary cooperation of members of the public in the investigation of a crime. "[L]aw enforcement officers do not violate the Fourth Amendment by merely approaching an individual on the street or in another public place, by asking him if he is willing to answer some questions, [or] by putting questions to him if the person is willing to listen." *Florida* v. *Royer*, 460 U.S. 491, 497, 103 S. Ct. 1319 (1983). See also ALI, Model Code of Pre–Arraignment Procedure § 110.1(1) (1975) ("[L]aw enforcement officer may . . . request any person to furnish information or otherwise cooperate in the investigation or prevention of crime"). That, in part, is because voluntary requests play a vital role in police investigatory work. See, *e.g., Haynes* v. *Washington*, 373 U.S. 503, 515, 83 S. Ct. 1336 (1963) ("[I]nterrogation of witnesses . . . is undoubtedly an essential tool in effective law enforcement"); U. S. Dept. of Justice, Eyewitness Evidence: A Guide for Law Enforcement 14–15 (1999) (instructing law enforcement to gather information from witnesses near the scene).

The importance of soliciting the public's assistance is offset to some degree by the need to stop a motorist to obtain that help—a need less likely present where a pedestrian, not a motorist, is involved. The difference is significant in light of our determinations that such an involuntary stop amounts to a "seizure" in Fourth Amendment terms. *E.g., Edmond* (cite omitted). That difference, however, is not important enough to justify an *Edmond*-type rule here. After all, as we have said, the motorist stop will likely be brief. Any accompanying traffic delay should prove no more onerous than many that typically accompany normal traffic congestion. And the resulting voluntary questioning of a motorist is as likely to prove important for police investigation as is the questioning of a pedestrian.

Given these considerations, it would seem anomalous were the law (1) ordinarily to allow police freely to seek the voluntary cooperation of pedestrians but (2) ordinarily to forbid police to seek similar voluntary cooperation from motorists.

Finally, we do not believe that an *Edmond*-type rule is needed to prevent an unreasonable proliferation of police checkpoints. Cf. *Lidster*, 202 Ill. 2d, at 9–10, 779 N. E. 2d, at 859–860 (expressing that concern). Practical considerations—namely, limited police resources and community hostility to related traffic tie-ups—seem likely to inhibit any such proliferation. See Fell, Ferguson, Williams, & Fields, Why Aren't Sobriety Checkpoints Widely Adopted as an Enforcement Strategy in the United States?, 35 Accident Analysis & Prevention 897 (Nov. 2003) (finding that sobriety checkpoints are not more widely used due to the lack of police resources and the lack of community support). And, of course, the Fourth Amendment's normal insistence that the stop be reasonable in context will still provide an important legal limitation on police use of this kind of information-seeking checkpoint.

These considerations, taken together, convince us that an *Edmond*-type presumptive rule of unconstitutionality does not apply here. That does not mean the stop is automatically, or even presumptively, constitutional. It simply means that we must judge its reasonableness, hence, its constitutionality, on the basis of the individual circumstances. And as this Court said in *Brown* v. *Texas,* 443 U.S. 47, 51, 99 S. Ct. 2637 (1979),"in judging reasonableness, we look to 'the gravity of the public concerns served by the seizure, the degree to which the seizure advances the public interest, and the severity of the interference with individual liberty.' " See also *Sitz, supra*, at 450–455, 110 S. Ct. 2481 (balancing these factors in determining reasonableness of a checkpoint stop) *Martinez-Fuerte* (cite omitted), (same).

III

We now consider the reasonableness of the checkpoint stop before us in light of the factors just mentioned, an issue that, in our view, has been fully argued here. We hold that the stop was constitutional.

The relevant public concern was grave. Police were investigating a crime that had resulted in a human death. No one denies the police's need to obtain more information at that time. And the stop's objective was to help find the perpetrator of a specific and known crime, not of unknown crimes of a general sort. Cf. *Edmond*, (cite omitted)

The stop advanced this grave public concern to a significant degree. The police appropriately tailored their checkpoint stops to fit important criminal investigatory needs. The stops took place about one week after the hit-and-run accident, on the same highway near the location of the accident, and at about the same time of night. And police used the stops to obtain information from drivers, some of whom might well have been in the vicinity of the crime at the time it occurred. See App. 28–29 (describing police belief that motorists routinely leaving work after night shifts at nearby industrial complexes might have seen something relevant).

Most importantly, the stops interfered only minimally with liberty of the sort the Fourth Amendment seeks to protect. Viewed objectively, each stop required only a brief wait in line—a very few minutes at most. Contact with the police lasted only a few seconds. Cf. *Martinez-Fuerte*, (cite omitted)(upholding stops of three-to-five minutes); *Sitz*, (cite omitted) (upholding delays of 25 seconds). Police contact consisted simply of a request for information and the distribution of a flyer. Cf. *Martinez-Fuerte* (cite omitted) (upholding inquiry as to motorists' citizenship and immigration status); *Sitz*, (cite omitted) (upholding examination of all drivers for signs of intoxication). Viewed subjectively, the contact provided little reason for anxiety or alarm. The police stopped all vehicles systematically. Cf. *Martinez-Fuerte*, (cite omitted); *Sitz*, (cite omitted). And there is no allegation here that the police acted in a discriminatory or otherwise unlawful manner while questioning motorists during stops.

For these reasons we conclude that the checkpoint stop was constitutional.

The judgment of the Illinois Supreme Court is reversed.

■ Concurring in part and dissenting in part: Justice Stevens, with whom Justice Souter and Justice Ginsburg join, concurring in part and dissenting in part.

There is a valid and important distinction between seizing a person to determine whether she has committed a crime and seizing a person to ask whether she has any information about an unknown person who committed a crime a week earlier. I therefore join Parts I and II of the Court's opinion explaining why our decision in *Indianapolis* v. *Edmond,* (cite omitted), is not controlling in this case. However, I find the issue discussed in Part III of the opinion closer than the Court does and believe it would be wise to remand the case to the Illinois state courts to address that issue in the first instance.

In contrast to pedestrians, who are free to keep walking when they encounter police officers handing out flyers or seeking information, motorists who confront a roadblock are required to stop, and to remain stopped for as long as the officers choose to detain them. Such a seizure may seem relatively innocuous to some, but annoying to others who are forced to wait for several minutes when the line of cars is lengthened—for example, by a surge of vehicles leaving a factory at the end of a shift. Still other drivers may find an unpublicized roadblock at midnight on a Saturday somewhat alarming.

On the other side of the equation, the likelihood that questioning a random sample of drivers will yield useful information about a hit-and-run accident that occurred a week earlier is speculative at best. To be sure, the sample in this case was not entirely random: The record reveals that the police knew that the victim had finished work at the Post Office shortly before the fatal accident, and hoped that other employees of the Post Office or the nearby industrial park might work on similar schedules and, thus, have been driving the same route at the same time the previous week. That is a plausible theory, but there is no evidence in the record that the police did anything to confirm that the nearby businesses in fact had shift changes at or near midnight on Saturdays, or that they had reason to believe that a roadblock would be more effective than, say, placing flyers on the employees' cars.

In short, the outcome of the multifactor test prescribed in *Brown* v. *Texas* (cite omitted), is by no means clear on the facts of this case. Because the Illinois Appellate Court and the State Supreme Court held that the Lombard roadblock was *per se* unconstitutional under *Indianapolis* v *Edmond*, neither court attempted to apply the *Brown* test. "We ordinarily do not decide in the first instance issues not resolved below." (cite omitted) We should be especially reluctant to abandon our role as a court of review in a case in which the constitutional inquiry requires analysis of local conditions and practices more familiar to judges closer to the scene. I would therefore remand the case to the Illinois courts to undertake the initial analysis of the issue that the Court resolves in Part III of its opinion. To that extent, I respectfully dissent.

M. BORDER AND IMMIGRATION SEARCHES

Add to end of first note on page 551 and before note 2:

Agents may conduct border searches without any probable cause or reasonable suspicion.

United States v. Manuel Flores–Montano

___ U.S. ___, 124 S.Ct. 1582 (March 30, 2004).

■ JUDGES: REHNQUIST, C. J., delivered the opinion for a unanimous Court. BREYER, J., filed a concurring opinion.

Customs officials seized 37 kilograms—a little more than 81 pounds—of marijuana from respondent Manuel Flores–Montano's gas tank at the international border. The Court of Appeals for the Ninth Circuit, relying on an earlier decision by a divided panel of that court, *United States* v. *Molina-Tarazon*, 279 F.3d 709 (2002), held that the Fourth Amendment forbade the fuel tank search absent reasonable suspicion (cite omitted). We hold that the search in question did not require reasonable suspicion.

Respondent, driving a 1987 Ford Taurus station wagon, attempted to enter the United States at the Otay Mesa Port of Entry in southern California. A customs inspector conducted an inspection of the station wagon, and requested respondent to leave the vehicle. The vehicle was then taken to a secondary inspection station.

At the secondary station, a second customs inspector inspected the gas tank by tapping it, and noted that the tank sounded solid. Subsequently, the inspector requested a mechanic under contract with Customs to come to the border station to remove the tank. Within 20 to 30 minutes, the mechanic arrived. He raised the car on a hydraulic lift, loosened the straps and unscrewed the bolts holding the gas tank to the undercarriage of the vehicle, and then disconnected some hoses and electrical connections. After the gas tank was removed, the inspector hammered off bondo (a putty-like hardening substance that is used to seal openings) from the top of the gas tank. The inspector opened an access plate underneath the bondo and found 37 kilograms of marijuana bricks. The process took 15 to 25 minutes.

A grand jury for the Southern District of California indicted respondent on one count of unlawfully importing marijuana, in violation of 21 U.S.C. § 952 [21 USCS § 952], and one count of possession of marijuana with intent to distribute, in violation of § 841(a)(1). Relying on *Molina-Tarazon*, respondent filed a motion to suppress the marijuana recovered from the gas tank. In *Molina-Tarazon*, a divided panel of the Court of Appeals held, *inter alia*, that removal of a gas tank requires reasonable suspicion in order to be consistent with the Fourth Amendment. 279 F.3d, at 717.

The Government advised the District Court that it was not relying on reasonable suspicion as a basis for denying respondent's suppression motion, but that it believed *Molina-Tarazon* was wrongly decided. The District Court, relying on *Molina-Tarazon*, held that reasonable suspicion was required to justify the search and, accordingly, granted respondent's motion to suppress. The Court of Appeals, citing *Molina-Tarazon*, summarily affirmed the District Court's judgment (cite omitted). We granted certiorari, (cite omitted), and now reverse.

In *Molina-Tarazon*, the Court of Appeals decided a case presenting similar facts to the one at bar. It asked "whether [the removal and dismantling of the defendant's fuel tank] is a 'routine' border search for which no suspicion whatsoever is required"(cite omitted). The Court of Appeals stated that "[i]n order to conduct a search that goes beyond the routine, an inspector must have reasonable suspicion," and the "critical factor" in determining whether a search is "routine" is the "degree of intrusiveness" (cite omitted).

The Court of Appeals seized on language from our opinion in *United States* v. *Montoya de Hernandez,* (cite omitted), in which we used the word "routine" as a descriptive term in discussing border searches (cite omitted).("Routine searches of the persons and effects of entrants are not subject to any requirement of reasonable suspicion, probable cause, or warrant"); (cite omitted) ("Because the issues are not presented today we suggest no view on what level of suspicion, if any, is required for nonroutine border searches such as strip, body-cavity, or involuntary x-ray searches"). The Court of Appeals took the term "routine," fashioned a new balancing test, and extended it to searches of vehicles. But the reasons that might support a requirement of some level of suspicion in the case of highly intrusive searches of the person—dignity and privacy interests of the person being searched—simply do not carry over to vehicles. Complex balancing tests to determine what is a "routine" search of a vehicle, as opposed to a more "intrusive" search of a person, have no place in border searches of vehicles.

The Government's interest in preventing the entry of unwanted persons and effects is at its zenith at the international border. Time and again, we have stated that "searches made at the border, pursuant to the longstanding right of the sovereign to protect itself by stopping and examining persons and property crossing into this country, are reasonable simply by virtue of the fact that they occur at the border." *United States* v. *Ramsey,* 431 U.S. 606, 616, 97 S. Ct. 1972 (1977). Congress, since the beginning of our Government, "has granted the Executive plenary authority to conduct routine searches and seizures at the border, without probable cause or a warrant, in order to regulate the collection of duties and to prevent the introduction of contraband into this country." *United States v. Montoya de Hernandez,* (citations omitted) The modern statute that authorized the search in this case, 46 Stat 747, 19 U.S.C. § 1581(a)[19 USCS § 1581(a)],[1] derived from a statute passed by the First Congress, the Act of Aug. 4, 1790, ch 35, § 31, 1 Stat 164, see *United States* v. *Villamonte-Marquez,* 462 U.S. 579, 584, 103 S. Ct. 2573 (1983), and reflects the "impressive historical pedigree" of the Government's power and interest, (citation omitted). It is axiomatic that the United States, as sovereign, has the inherent authority to protect, and a paramount interest in protecting, its territorial integrity.

That interest in protecting the borders is illustrated in this case by the evidence that smugglers frequently attempt to penetrate our borders with contraband secreted in their automobiles' fuel tank. Over the past 5 1/2 fiscal years, there have been 18,788 vehicle drug seizures at the southern California ports of entry. App. to Pet. for Cert. 12a. Of those 18,788, gas tank drug seizures have accounted for 4,619 of the vehicle drug seizures, or approximately 25%. *Ibid.* In addition, instances of persons smuggled in and around gas tank compartments are discovered at the ports of entry of San Ysidro and Otay Mesa at a rate averaging 1 approximately every 10 days. (cite omitted).

Respondent asserts two main arguments with respect to his Fourth Amendment interests. First, he urges that he has a privacy interest in his fuel tank, and that the suspicion less disassembly of his tank is an invasion of his privacy. But on many occasions, we have noted that "the expectation of privacy is less at the border than it is in the interior." *Montoya de Hernandez,* (cite omitted). We have long recognized that automobiles seeking entry into this country may be searched. See *Carroll* v. *United States,* 267 U.S. 132, 154, 45 S. Ct. 280 (1925) ("Travellers may be so stopped in crossing an international boundary because of national self protection reasonably requiring one entering the country to identify himself as entitled to come in, and his belongings as effects which may be lawfully brought in"). It is difficult to imagine how the search of a gas tank, which should be solely a repository for fuel, could be more of an invasion of privacy than the search of the automobile's passenger compartment.

Second, respondent argues that the Fourth Amendment "protects property as well as privacy," *Soldal* v. *Cook County,* 506 U.S. 56, 62, 113 S. Ct. 538 (1992), and that the disassembly and reassembly of his gas tank is a significant deprivation of his property interest because it may damage the

1. Section 1581(a) provides: "Any officer of the customs may at any time go on board of any vessel or vehicle at any place in the United States or within the customs waters or, as he may be authorized, within a customs-enforcement area established under the Anti–Smuggling Act, or at any other authorized place, without as well as within his district, and examine the manifest and other documents and papers and examine, inspect, and search the vessel or vehicle and every part thereof and any person, trunk, package, or cargo on board, and to this end may hail and stop such vessel or vehicle, and use all necessary force to compel compliance."

vehicle. He does not, and on the record cannot, truly contend that the procedure of removal, disassembly, and reassembly of the fuel tank in this case or any other has resulted in serious damage to, or destruction of, the property.[2] According to the Government, for example, in fiscal year 2003, 348 gas tank searches conducted along the southern border were negative (*i.e.*, no contraband was found), the gas tanks were reassembled, and the vehicles continued their entry into the United States without incident. Brief for United States 31.

Respondent cites not a single accident involving the vehicle or motorist in the many thousands of gas tank disassemblies that have occurred at the border. A gas tank search involves a brief procedure that can be reversed without damaging the safety or operation of the vehicle. If damage to a vehicle were to occur, the motorist might be entitled to recovery. While the interference with a motorist's possessory interest is not insignificant when the Government removes, disassembles, and reassembles his gas tank, it nevertheless is justified by the Government's paramount interest in protecting the border.[3]

For the reasons stated, we conclude that "the Government's authority to conduct suspicionless inspections at the border includes the authority to remove, disassemble, and reassemble a vehicle's fuel tank." While it may be true that some searches of property are so destructive as to require a different result, this was not one of them. The judgment of the United States Court of Appeals for the Ninth Circuit is therefore reversed, and the case is remanded for further proceedings consistent with this opinion.

It is so ordered.

■ CONCUR: JUSTICE BREYER, CONCURRING.

I join the Court's opinion in full. I also note that Customs keeps track of the border searches its agents conduct, including the reasons for the searches. Tr. of Oral Arg. 53–54. This administrative process should help minimize concerns that gas tank searches might be undertaken in an abusive manner.

2. Respondent's reliance on cases involving exploratory drilling searches is misplaced. See *United States* v. *Rivas*, 157 F.3d 364 (CA5 1998) (drilling into body of trailer required reasonable suspicion); *United States* v. *Robles*, 45 F.3d 1 (CA1 1995) (drilling into machine part required reasonable suspicion); *United States* v. Carreon, 872 F.2d 1436 (CA10 1989) (drilling into camper required reasonable suspicion). We have no reason at this time to pass on the reasonableness of drilling, but simply note the obvious factual difference that this case involves the procedure of removal, disassembly, and reassembly of a fuel tank, rather than potentially destructive drilling. We again leave open the question "whether, and under what circumstances, a border search might be deemed 'unreasonable' because of the particularly offensive manner it is carried out." *United States v. Ramsey* (cite omitted).

3. Respondent also argued that he has some sort of Fourth Amendment right not to be subject to delay at the international border and that the need for the use of specialized labor, as well as the hour actual delay here and the potential for even greater delay for reassembly are an invasion of that right. Respondent points to no cases indicating the Fourth Amendment shields entrants from inconvenience or delay at the international border.

The procedure in this case took about an hour (including the wait for the mechanic). At oral argument, the Government advised us that, depending on the type of car, a search involving the disassembly and reassembly of a gas tank may take one to two hours. Tr. of Oral Arg. 10. We think it clear that delays of one to two hours at international borders are to be expected.

CHAPTER 6

Exclusionary Principles & Alternative Remedies

C. The Good-Faith Exception

Add after note 1 on page 598:

In a more recent case, the Court rejected a good faith exception argument and held that evidence seized on the basis of a facially deficient warrant violated the Fourth Amendment:

Groh v. Ramirez

540 U.S. ___, 124 S.Ct. 1284 (February 24, 2004)

■ Justice Stevens delivered the opinion of the Court.

Petitioner conducted a search of respondents' home pursuant to a warrant that failed to describe the "persons or things to be seized." U.S. Const., Amdt 4. The questions presented are (1) whether the search violated the Fourth Amendment, and (2) if so, whether petitioner nevertheless is entitled to qualified immunity, given that a Magistrate Judge (Magistrate), relying on an affidavit that particularly described the items in question, found probable cause to conduct the search.

I

Respondents, Joseph Ramirez and members of his family, live on a large ranch in Butte–Silver Bow County, Montana. Petitioner, Jeff Groh, has been a Special Agent for the Bureau of Alcohol, Tobacco and Firearms (ATF) since 1989. In February 1997, a concerned citizen informed petitioner that on a number of visits to respondents' ranch the visitor had seen a large stock of weaponry, including an automatic rifle, grenades, a grenade launcher, and a rocket launcher. Based on that information, petitioner prepared and signed an application stated that the search was for "any automatic firearms or parts to automatic weapons, destructive devices to include but not limited to grenades, grenade launchers, rocket launchers, and any and all receipts pertaining to the purchase or manufacture of automatic weapons or explosive devices or launchers." Petitioner supported the application with a detailed affidavit, which he also prepared and executed, that set forth the basis for his belief that the listed items were concealed on the ranch. Petitioner then presented these documents to a Magistrate, along with a warrant form that petitioner also had completed. The Magistrate signed the warrant form.

Although the application particularly described the place to be searched and the contraband petitioner expected to find, the warrant itself was less specific; it failed to identify any of the items that petitioner intended to seize. In the portion of the form that called for a description of the "person or property" to be seized, petitioner typed a description of respondents' two-story blue house rather than the alleged stockpile of firearms.[1] The warrant did not incorporate by reference the itemized list contained in the application. It did, however, recite that the Magistrate was satisfied the affidavit established probable cause to believe that contraband was concealed on the premises, and that sufficient grounds existed for the warrant's issuance.[2]

The day after the Magistrate issued the warrant, petitioner led a team of law enforcement officers, including both federal agents and members of the local sheriff's department, in the search of respondents' premises. Although respondent Joseph Ramirez was not home, his wife and children were. Petitioner states that he orally described the objects of the search to Mrs. Ramirez in person and to Mr. Ramirez by telephone. According to Mrs. Ramirez, however, petitioner explained only that he was searching for "an explosive device in a box." Ramirez v. Butte–Silver Bow County,298 F.3d 1022, 1026 (CA2002). At any rate, the officers' search uncovered no illegal weapons or explosives. When the officers left, petitioner gave Mrs. Ramirez a copy of the search warrant, but not a copy of the application, which had been sealed. The following day, in response to a request from respondents' attorney, petitioner faxed the attorney a copy of the page of the application that listed the items to be seized. No charges were filed against the Ramirezes.

Respondents sued petitioner and the other officers under *Bivens v. Six Unknown Fed. Narcotics Agents*, 403 U.S. 388, 91 S.Ct. 1999 (1971) raising eight claims, including violation of the Fourth Amendment. The District Court entered summary judgment for all defendants. The court found on the Fourth Amendment violation, because it considered the case comparable to one in which the warrant contained an inaccurate address, and in such a case, the court reasoned, the warrant is sufficiently detailed if the executing officers can locate the correct house. The court added that even if a constitutional violation occurred, the defendants were entitled to qualified immunity because the failure of the warrant to describe the objects of the search amounted to a mere "typographical error."

The Court of Appeals affirmed the judgment with respect to all defendants and all claims, with respect to all defendants and all claims, with the exception of respondents' Fourth Amendment claim against petitioner. On that claim, the court held that the warrant was invalid because it did not "describe with particularity the place to be searched and the items to be seized," and that oral statements by petitioner during or after the search could not cure the omission. The court observed that the

1. The warrant stated: "[T]here is now concealed [on the specified premise] a certain person or property, namely [a] single dwelling residence two story in height which is blue in color and has two additions attached to the east. The front entrance to the residence faces in a southerly direction." App. To Pet. for Cert. 26a.

2. The affidavit was sealed. Its sufficiency is not disputed.

warrant's facial defect "increased the likelihood and degree of confrontation between Ramirezes and the police" and deprived respondents of the means "to challenge officers who might have exceeded the limits imposed by the magistrate." The court also expressed concern that "permitting officers to expand the scope of the warrant by oral statements would broaden the area of dispute between the parties in subsequent litigation." The court nevertheless concluded that all of the officers except petitioner were protected by qualified immunity. With respect to petitioner, the court read our opinion in *United States v. Leon*, 468 U.S. 897, 104 S.Ct. 3405 (1984) as precluding qualified immunity for the leader of a search who fails to "read the warrant and satisfy [himself] that [he] understand[s] its scope and limitations, and it is not defective in some obvious way." The court added that "[t]he leaders of the search team must also make sure that a copy of the warrant is available to give to the person whose property is being searched at the commencement of the search, and that such copy has no missing pages or other obvious defects" (cites omitted).

II

The warrant was plainly invalid. The Fourth Amendment states unambiguously that "no Warrants shall issue, but upon probable cause, supported by Oath or affirmation, and particularly describing the place to be searched, and *the persons or things to be seized*." (Emphasis added.) The warrant in this case complied with the first three of these requirements: It is based on probable cause and supported by a sworn affidavit, and it described particularly the place of the search. On the fourth requirement, however, the warrant failed altogether. Indeed, petitioner concedes that "the warrant ... was deficient in particularity because it provided no description of the type of evidence sought." Brief for Petitioner 10.

The fact that the application adequately described the "things to be seized" does not save the *warrant* from its facial invalidity. The Fourth Amendment by its terms requires particularity in the warrant, not in the supporting documents. See *Massachusetts v. Sheppard*, 468 U.S. 981, 104 S.Ct. 3424 (1984) ("[A] warrant that fails to conform to the particularity requirement of the Fourth Amendment is unconstitutional").... But in case the warrant did not incorporate other documents by reference, nor did either the affidavit or the application (which had been placed under seal) accompany the warrant. Hence, we need not further explore the matter of incorporation.

Petitioner argues that even though the warrant was invalid, the search nevertheless was "reasonable" within the meaning of the Fourth Amendment. He notes that a Magistrate authorized the search on the basis of adequate evidence of probable cause, that petitioner orally described to respondents the items to be seized, and that the search did not exceed the limits intended by the Magistrate and described by petitioner. Thus, petitioner maintains, his search of respondents' ranch was functionally equivalent to a search authorized by a valid warrant.

We disagree. This warrant did not simply omit a few items from a list of many to be seized, or misdescribe a few of several items. Nor did it make what fairly could be characterized as a mere technical mistake or typographical error. Rather, in the space set aside for a description of the items to be seized, the warrant stated that the items consisted of a "single dwelling residence ... blue in color." In other words, the warrant did not describe the items to be seized *at* all (emphasis in original). In this respect the warrant was so obviously deficient that we must regard the search as "warrantless" within the meaning of our case law (cites omitted). Our cases have firmly established the "basic principle of Fourth Amendment law that searches and seizures inside a home without a warrant are presumptively unreasonable," *Payton v. New York*, 445 U.S. 573, 586, 100 S.Ct. 1371 (1980) (footnote omitted).... Thus, "absent exigent circumstances, a warrantless entry to search for weapons or contraband is unconstitutional even when a felony has been committed and there is probable cause to believe that incriminating evidence will be found within." *Id.*, 445 U.S. at 587–88, 1010 S.Ct. 1371 (footnote omitted) (further cites omitted).

We have clearly stated that the presumptive rule against warrantless searches applies with equal force to searches whose only defect is a lack of particularity in the warrant. In *Sheppard,* for instance, the petitioner argued that even though the warrant was invalid for lack of particularity, "the search was constitutional because it was reasonable within the meaning of the Fourth Amendment." 468 U.S., at 988, n. 5. In squarely rejecting that position, we explained:

> The uniformly applied rule is that a search conducted pursuant to a warrant that fails to conform to the particularity requirement of the Fourth Amendment is unconstitutional. (cites omitted). That rule is in keeping with the well-established principle that 'except in certain carefully defined classes of cases, a search of private property without proper consent is "unreasonable" unless it has been authorized by a valid search warrant' (cites omitted).

Petitioner asks us to hold that a search conducted pursuant to a warrant lacking particularity should be exempt from the presumption of unreasonableness if the goals served by the particularity requirement are otherwise satisfied. He maintains that the requirement are otherwise satisfied. He maintains that the search in this case satisfied those goals–which he says are "to prevent general searches, to prevent the seizure of one thing under a warrant describing another, and to prevent warrants from being issued o vague or dubious information ," Brief for Petitioner 16–because the scope of the search did not exceed the limits set forth in the application. But unless the particular items described in the affidavit are also set forth in the warrant itself (or at least incorporated by reference, and the affidavit present at the search), there can be no written assurance that the Magistrate actually found probable cause to search for, and to seize, every item mentioned in the affidavit (cite omitted). In this case, for example, it is at least theoretically possible that the Magistrate was satisfied that the search for weapons and explosives was justified by the showing in the affidavit, but not convinced that any evidentiary basis existed for rummaging through respondents' files and papers for receipts pertaining to the purchase or manufacture of such items. Cf. *Stanford* v. *Texas,* 379 U.S. 476, 485–486, 85 S. Ct. 506 (1965). Or, conceivably, the Magistrate might have believed that some of the weapons mentioned in the affidavit could have been lawfully possessed and therefore should not be seized. See 26 USC § 5861 [26 USCS § 5861] (requiring registration, but not banning possession of, certain firearms). The mere fact that the Magistrate issued a warrant does not necessarily establish that he agreed that the scope of the search should be as broad as the affiant's request. Even though petitioner acted with restraint in conducting the search, "the inescapable fact is that this restraint was imposed by the agents themselves, not by a judicial officer." *Katz* v. *United States,* 389 U.S. 347, 356, 88 S. Ct. 507 (1967).[3]

We have long held, moreover, that the purpose of the particularity requirement is not limited to the prevention of general searches (cite omitted). A particular warrant also "assures the individual whose property is searched or seized of the lawful authority of the executing officer, his need to search, and the limits of his power to search"(cites omitted)....

It is incumbent on the officer executing a search warrant to ensure the search is lawfully authorized and lawfully conducted. Because petitioner did not have in his possession a warrant particularly describing the things he intended to seize, proceeding with the search was clearly "unreasonable" under the Fourth Amendment. The Court of Appeals correctly held that the search was unconstitutional.

III

Having concluded that a constitutional violation occurred, we turn to the question whether petitioner is entitled to qualified immunity despite that violation. See *Wilson* v. *Layne,* 526 U.S. 603, 609, 119 S. Ct. 1692 (1999). The answer depends on whether the right that was transgressed was " 'clearly established' "—that is, "whether it would be clear to a reasonable officer that his conduct was unlawful in the situation he confronted." *Saucier* v. *Katz,* 533 U.S. 194, 202, 150 L. Ed. 2d 272, 121 S. Ct. 2151 (2001). Given that the particularity requirement is set forth in the text of the Constitution, no reasonable officer could believe that a warrant that plainly did not comply with that requirement was valid. See *Harlow* v. *Fitzgerald,* 457 U.S. 800, 818–819, 102 S. Ct. 2727 (1982) ("If the law was clearly established, the immunity defense ordinarily should fail, since a reasonably competent public official should know the law governing his conduct"). Moreover, because petitioner himself prepared the invalid warrant, he may not argue that he reasonably relied on the Magistrate's

3. For this reason petitioner's argument that any constitutional error was committed by the Magistrate, not petitioner, is misplaced. In *Massachusetts v. Sheppard*, 468 U.S. 981, 104 S. Ct. 3424 (1984), we suggested that "the judge, not the police officers," may have committed "[a]n error of constitutional dimension," *id.*, 468 U.S. at 990, 104 S. Ct. 3424, because the judge had assured the officers requesting the warrant that he would take the steps necessary to conform the warrant to constitutional requirements, *id.*, 468 U.S. at 968, 104 S. Ct. 3424. Thus, "it was not unreasonable for the police in [that] case to rely on the judge's assurances that the warrant authorized the search they had requested." *id.*, 468 U.S. at 900, n. 6, 1024 S. Ct. 3424. In this case, by contrast, the petitioner did not alert the Magistrate to the defect in the warrant the petitioner had drafted, and we therefore cannot know whether the Magistrate was aware of the search he was authorizing. Nor would it have been reasonable for petitioner to rely on a warrant that was so patently defective, even if the Magistrate was aware of the deficiency. See United States v. Leon, 468 U.S. 897, 915, 922, n. 23, 104 S. Ct. 3405 (1984).

assurance that the warrant contained an adequate description of the things to be seized and was therefore valid. Cf. *Sheppard*, 468 U.S., at 989–990, 104 S. Ct. 3424. In fact, the guidelines of petitioner's own department placed him on notice that he might be liable for executing a manifestly invalid warrant. An ATF directive in force at the time of this search warned: "Special agents are liable if they exceed their authority while executing a search warrant and must be sure that a search warrant is sufficient on its face even when issued by a magistrate." Searches and Examinations, ATF Order O 3220.1(7)(d) (Feb. 13, 1997). See also *id.,* at 3220.1(23)(b) ("If any error or deficiency is discovered and there is a reasonable probability that it will invalidate the warrant, such warrant shall not be executed. The search shall be postponed until a satisfactory warrant has been obtained").[4] And even a cursory reading of the warrant in this case—perhaps just a simple glance—would have revealed a glaring deficiency that any reasonable police officer would have known was constitutionally fatal.

No reasonable officer could claim to be unaware of the basic rule, well established by our cases, that, absent consent or exigency, a warrantless search of the home is presumptively unconstitutional. See *Payton*, 445 U.S., at 586–588, 100 S. Ct. 1371. Indeed, as we noted nearly 20 years ago in *Sheppard:* "The uniformly applied rule is that a search conducted pursuant to a warrant that fails to conform to the particularity requirement of the Fourth Amendment is unconstitutional." 468 U.S., at 988, n. 5, 104 S. Ct. 3424.[5] Because not a word in any of our cases would suggest to a reasonable officer that this case fits within any exception to that fundamental tenet, petitioner is asking us, in effect, to craft a new exception. Absent any support for such an exception in our cases, he cannot reasonably have relied on an expectation that we would do so.

Petitioner contends that the search in this case was the product, at worst, of a lack of due care, and that our case law requires more than negligent behavior before depriving an official of qualified immunity. See *Malley* v. *Briggs,* 475 U.S. 335, 341, 106 S. Ct. 1092 (1986). But as we observed in the companion case to *Sheppard*, "a warrant may be so facially deficient—*i.e.*, in failing to particularize the place to be searched or the things to be seized—that the executing officers cannot reasonably presume it to be valid." *Leon,* 468 U.S., at 923, 104 S. Ct. 3405 . This is such a case.[6]

4. We do not suggest that an official is deprived of qualified immunity whenever he violates an internal guideline. We refer to the ATF Order only to underscore that petitioner should have known that he should not execute a patently defective warrant.

5. Although both *Sheppard* and *Leon* involved the application of the "good faith" exception to the Fourth Amendment's general exclusionary rule, we have explained that "the same standard of objective reasonableness that we applied in the context of a suppression hearing in *Leon* defines the qualified immunity accorded an officer." *Malley* v. *Briggs,* 475 U.S. 335, 344, 106 S. Ct. 1092 (1986) (citation omitted).

6. Justice Kennedy argues in dissent that we have not allowed " 'ample room for mistaken judgments,' " *post*, at ___, 157 L. Ed. 2d, at 1087 (quoting *Malley*, 475 U.S., at 343, 271, 106S. Ct. 1092), because "difficult and important tasks demand the officer's full attention in the heat of an ongoing and often dangerous criminal investigation." In this case, however, petitioner does not contend that any sort of exigency existed when he drafted the affidavit, the warrant application, and the warrant, or when he conducted the

Accordingly, the judgment of the Court of Appeals is affirmed.

It is so ordered.

■ DISSENT: JUSTICE KENNEDY, with whom the CHIEF JUSTICE joins, dissenting.

I agree with the Court that the Fourth Amendment was violated in this case. The Fourth Amendment states that "no Warrants shall issue, but upon probable cause, supported by Oath or affirmation, and particularly describing the place to be search, and the persons or things to be seized." The warrant issued in this case did not particularly describe the things to be seized, and so did not comply with the Fourth Amendment. I disagree with the Court on whether the officer who obtained the warrant and led the search team is entitled to qualified immunity for his role in the search. In my view, the officer should receive qualified immunity.

The present case involves a straightforward mistake of fact. Although the Court does not acknowledge it directly, it is obvious from the record below that the officer simply made a clerical error when he filled out the proposed warrant and offered it to the Magistrate Judge. The officer used the proper description of the property to be seized when he completed the affidavit. He also used the proper description in the accompanying application. When he typed up the description a third time for the proposed warrant, however, the officer accidentally entered a description of the place to be searched in the part of the warrant form that called for a description of the property to be seized. No one noticed the error before the search was executed. Although the record is not entirely clear on this point, the mistake apparently remained undiscovered until the day after the search when respondents' attorney reviewed the warrant for defects. The officer, being unaware of his mistake, did not rely on it in any way. It is uncontested that the officer trained the search team and executed the warrant based on his mistaken belief that the warrant contained the proper description of the items to be seized.

The question is whether the officer's mistaken belief that the warrant contained the proper language was a reasonable belief. In my view, it was. A law enforcement officer charged with leading a team to execute a search warrant for illegal weapons must fulfill a number of serious responsibilities. The officer must establish probable cause to believe the crime has been committed and that evidence is likely to be found at the place to be search; must articulate specific items that can be seized, and a specific place to be searched; must obtain the warrant from a magistrate judge; and must instruct a search team to execute the warrant within the time allowed by the warrant. The officer must also oversee the execution of the warrant in

search. This is not the situation, therefore, in which we have recognized that "officers in the dangerous and difficult process of making arrests and executing search warrants" require "some latitude." *Maryland* v. *Garrison*, 480 U.S. 79, 87, 107 S. Ct. 1013 (1987).

Nor are we according "the correctness of paper forms" a higher status than "substantive rights." As we have explained, the Fourth Amendment's particularity requirement assures the subject of the search that a magistrate has duly authorized the officer to conduct a search of limited scope. This substantive right is not protected when the officer fails to take the time to glance at the authorizing document and detect a glaring defect that Justice Kennedy agrees is of constitutional magnitude.

a way that protects officer safety, directs a thorough and professional search for the evidence, and avoids unnecessary destruction of property. These difficult and important tasks demand the officer's full attention in the heat of an ongoing and often dangerous criminal investigation.

An officer who complies fully with all of these duties can be excused for not being aware that he had made a clerical error in the course of filling out the proposed warrant. See *Maryland v. Garrison,* 480 U.S. 79, 87, 107 S. Ct 1013 (1987) (recognizing "the need to allow some latitude for honest mistakes that are made by officers in the dangerous and difficult process of making arrests and executing search warrants"). An officer who drafts an affidavit, types up an application and proposed warrant, and then obtains a judge's approval naturally assumes that he has filled out the warrant form correctly. Even if the officer checks over the warrant, he may very well miss a mistake. We all tend toward myopia when looking for our own errors. Every lawyer and every judge can recite examples of documents that they wrote, checked, and double checked, but that still contained glaring errors. Law enforcement officers are no different. It would be better if the officer recognizes the error, of course. It would be better still if he does not make the mistake in the first place. In the context of an otherwise proper search, however, and officer's failure to recognize his clerical error on a warrant form can be a reasonable mistake.

■ JUSTICE THOMAS with whom JUSTICE SCALIA joins, and with whom THE CHIEF JUSTICE joins as to Part III, dissenting.

The Fourth Amendment provides: "The right of the people to be secure in their persons, houses, and papers, and effects, against unreasonable searches and seizures, shall not be violated, and no Warrants shall issue, but upon probable cause, supported by Oath or affirmation, and the persons or things to be seized." The precise relationship between the Amendment's Warrant Clause and Unreasonableness Clause is unclear. But neither Clause explicitly requires a warrant. While "it is of course textually possible to consider [a warrant requirement] implicit within the requirement of reasonableness," California v. Acevedo, 500 U.S. 565, 582, 111. Ct. 1982 (1991) (Scalia, J., concurring in judgment), the text of the Fourth Amendment certainly does not mandate this result. Nor does the Amendment's history, which is clear as to the Amendment's principal target (general warrants), but not as clear with respect to when warrants were required, if ever. Indeed, because of the very different nature and scope of federal authority and ability to conduct searches and arrests at the founding, it is possible that neither the history of the Fourth Amendment nor the common law provides much guidance.

As a result, the Court has vacillated between imposing a categorical warrant requirement and applying a general reasonableness standard. That is, our cases stand for the illuminating proposition that warrantless searches are *per se* unreasonable, except, of course, when they are not.

Today the Court holds that the warrant in this case was "so obvious deficient" that the ensuing search must be regarded as a warrantless search and thus presumptively unreasonable. However, the text of the Fourth Amendment, its history, and the sheer number of exceptions to Court's categorical warrant requirement seriously undermine the bases upon which the Court today rests its holding. Instead of adding to this confusing jurisprudence, as the Court has done, I would turn to first principles in order to determine the relationship between the Warrant Clause and the Unreasonableness Clause. But even within the Court's current framework, a search conducted pursuant to a "warrantless search." Consequently, despite the defective warrant, I would still ask whether this search was unreasonable and would conclude that it was not. Furthermore, even if the Court were correct that this search violated the Constitution (and in particular, respondents' Fourth Amendment rights), given the confused state of our Fourth Amendment jurisprudence and the reasonableness of petitioner's actions, I cannot agree with the Court's conclusion that petitioner is not entitled to qualified immunity. For these reasons, I respectfully dissent.

I

"[A]ny Fourth Amendment case may present two separate questions: whether the search was conducted pursuant to a warrant issued in accordance with the second Clause, and, if not, whether it was nevertheless 'reasonable' within the meaning of the first." United States v. Leon, 468 U.S. 897, 961, 104 S. Ct. 3405 (1984) (Stevens, J. Dissenting). By categorizing the search here to be a "warrantless" one, the Court declines to perform a reasonableness inquiry and ignore the fact that this search is quite different from searches that the Court has considered to be "warrantless" in the past. Our cases involving "warrantless" searches do not generally involve situations in which an officer has obtained a warrant that is later determined to be facially defective, but rather involve situations in which the officers neither sought nor obtained a warrant. By simply treating this case as if no warrant had even been sought or issued, the Court glosses over what should be the key inquiry: whether it is always appropriate to treat a search made pursuant to a warrant that fails to describe particularly the things to be seized as presumptively unreasonable.

In the instant case, the items to be seized were clearly specified in the warrant application and set forth in the affidavit, both of which were given to the Judge (Magistrate). The Magistrate reviewed all of the documents and signed the warrant application. It is clear that respondents here received the protection of the Warrant Clause, as described in *Johnson* and *McDonald*. Under these circumstances, I would not hold that any ensuing search constitutes a presumptively unreasonable warrantless search. Instead, I would determine whether , despite the invalid warrant, the resulting search was reasonable and hence constitutional.

II

Because the search was not unreasonable, I would conclude that it was constitutional. Prior to execution of the warrant, petitioner briefed the search team and provided a copy of the search warrant application, the supporting affidavit, and the warrant for the officers to review. Petitioner orally reviewed the terms of the warrant with the officers, including the specific items for which the officers were authorized to search. Petitioner and his search team then conducted the search entirely within the scope of the warrant application and warrant that is, within the scope of what the

Magistrate had authorized. Finding no illegal weapons or explosives, the search team seized nothing.

The only remaining question is whether petitioner's failure to notice the defect was objectively unreasonable. The Court today points to no cases directing an officer to proofread a warrant after it has been passed on by a neutral magistrate, where the officer is already fully aware of the scope of the intended search and the magistrate gives no reason to believe that he has authorized anything other than the requested search. Nor does the Court point to any case suggesting that where the same officer both prepares and executes the invalid warrant, he can never rely on the magistrate's assurance that the warrant is proper. Indeed, in *Massachusetts v. Sheppard*, 468 U.S. 981, 104 S. Ct. 3424 (1984), The Court suggested that although an officer who is not involved in the warrant application process would normally read the issued warrant to determine the object of the search, an executing officer who is also the affiant might not need to do so. *Id.*, 468 U.S. at 989, n. 6, 104 S. Ct. 3424.

Although the Court contends that it does not impose a proofreading requirement upon officers executing warrants, I see no other way to read its decision, particularly where, as here, petitioner could have done nothing more to ensure the reasonableness of his actions than to proofread the warrant. After receiving several allegations that respondents possessed illegal firearms and explosives, petitioner prepared an application for a warrant to search respondents' ranch, along with a supporting affidavit detailing the history of allegations against respondents, petitioner's investigation into these allegations, and petitioner's verification of the sources of the allegations. Petitioner properly filled out the warrant application, which described both the place to be search and the things to be seized, and obtained the Magistrate's signature on both the warrant application and the warrant itself. Prior to execution of the warrant, petitioner briefed the search team to ensure that each officer understood the limits of the search. Petitioner and his search team then executed the warrant within those limits. And when the error in the search warrant was discovered, petitioner promptly faxed the missing information to respondents. In my view, petitioner's actions were objectively reasonable, and thus he should be entitled to qualified immunity.

D. ALTERNATIVE REMEDIES

Add after note 1 on page 608:

For another variation on the sovereign immunity theme, see *Inyo County v. Paiute–Shoshone Indians of the Bishop Community of the Bishop Colony*, 538 U.S. 701, 123 S.Ct. 1887 (2003). In dicta, the Court indicated that Indian tribes, like States, are not "persons" subject to suits under 42 U.S.C. § 1983. Moreover, the tribe sought to interpose 42 U.S.C. § 1983 as a claimant to argue it was immune from the execution of a search. The Court determined that, in the situation presented, the Tribe did not qualify as a person within the jurisdiction of the United States under § 1983. The Tribe could not sue under § 1983 to vindicate the sovereign right it claimed. Section 1983 was designed to secure private rights against government encroachment, not to advance a sovereign's prerogative to withhold evidence relevant to a criminal investigation.

Add at the end of note 3 on page 608:

Would this explain the difference in the Court's approach to the facts in *Massachusetts v. Sheppard*, 468 U.S. 981, 104 S.Ct. 3424 (1984) [described in note 1 on page 598 *supra*] as compared to the Court's approach to the facts in *Groh v. Ramirez*, 540 U.S. ___, 124 S.Ct. 1284 (2004) [added in this supplement to note 1 on page 598]?

G. DERIVATIVE EVIDENCE: PRINCIPLES AND LIMITATIONS

Add after first paragraph of note 3 on page 666:

If officers fail to give *Miranda* warnings to a suspect in a situation in which they are required (custodial interrogation), but the suspect nevertheless makes a voluntary statement that leads to the discovery of physical evidence, must the physical evidence be suppressed?:

United States v. Patane

___ U.S. ___, 124 S.Ct. 2620 (June 28, 2004).

■ OPINION: JUSTICE THOMAS announced the judgment of the Court and delivered an opinion, in which THE CHIEF JUSTICE and JUSTICE SCALIA join.

In this case we must decide whether a failure to give a suspect the warnings prescribed by *Miranda* v. *Arizona,* 384 U.S. 436, 86 S. Ct. 1602 (1966), requires suppression of the physical fruits of the suspect's unwarned but voluntary statements. The Court has previously addressed this question but has not reached a definitive conclusion. See *Massachusetts* v. *White,* 439 U.S. 280, 99 S. Ct. 712 (1978) *(per curiam)* (dividing evenly on the question); see also *Patterson* v. *United States*, 485 U.S. 922, 108 S. Ct. 1093 (1988) (White, J., dissenting from denial of certiorari). Although we believe that the Court's decisions in *Oregon* v. *Elstad,* 470 U.S. 298, 105 S. Ct. 1285 (1985), and *Michigan* v. *Tucker,* 417 U.S. 433, 94 S. Ct. 2357 (1974), are instructive, the Courts of Appeals have split on the question after our decision in *Dickerson* v. *United States,* 530 U.S. 428, 120 S. Ct. 2326 (2000). See, *e.g., United States* v. *Villalba-Alvarado*, 345 F.3d 1007 (8th Cir. 2003) (holding admissible the physical fruits of a *Miranda* violation); *United States* v. *Sterling*, 283 F.3d 216 (4th Cir. 2002) (same); *United States* v. *DeSumma*, 272 F.3d 176 (CA3 2001) (same); *United States* v. *Faulkingham,* 295 F.3d 85 (1st Cir. 2002) (holding admissible the physical fruits of a negligent *Miranda* violation). Because the *Miranda* rule protects against violations of the Self–Incrimination Clause, which, in turn, is not implicated by the introduction at trial of physical evidence resulting from voluntary statements, we answer the question presented in the negative.

I

In June 2001, respondent, Samuel Francis Patane, was arrested for harassing his ex-girlfriend, Linda O'Donnell. He was released on bond, subject to a temporary restraining order that prohibited him from contacting O'Donnell. Respondent apparently violated the restraining order by attempting to telephone O'Donnell. On June 6, 2001, Officer Tracy Fox of the Colorado Springs Police Department began to investigate the matter. On the same day, a county probation officer informed an agent of the Bureau of Alcohol, Tobacco, and Firearms (ATF), that respondent, a convicted felon, illegally possessed a .40 Glock pistol. The ATF relayed this information to Detective Josh Benner, who worked closely with the ATF. Together, Detective Benner and Officer Fox proceeded to respondent's residence.

After reaching the residence and inquiring into respondent's attempts to contact O'Donnell, Officer Fox arrested respondent for violating the restraining order. Detective Benner attempted to advise respondent of his *Miranda* rights but got no further than the right to remain silent. At that point, respondent interrupted, asserting that he knew his rights, and neither officer attempted to complete the warning.[1] App. 40.

Detective Benner then asked respondent about the Glock. Respondent was initially reluctant to discuss the matter, stating: "I am not sure I should tell you anything about the Glock because I don't want you to take it away from me." Detective Benner persisted, and respondent told him that the pistol was in his bedroom. Respondent then gave Detective Benner permission to retrieve the pistol. Detective Benner found the pistol and seized it.

A grand jury indicted respondent for possession of a firearm by a convicted felon, in violation of 18 U.S.C. § 922(g)(1). The District Court granted respondent's motion to suppress the firearm, reasoning that the officers lacked probable cause to arrest respondent for violating the restraining order. It therefore declined to rule on respondent's alternative argument that the gun should be suppressed as the fruit of an unwarned statement.

The Court of Appeals reversed the District Court's ruling with respect to probable cause but affirmed the suppression order on respondent's alternative theory. The court rejected the Government's argument that this Court's decisions in *Elstad, supra,* and Tucker, supra, foreclosed application of the fruit of the poisonous tree doctrine of *Wong Sun* v. *United States,* 371 U.S. 471, 83 S. Ct. 407 (1963), to the present context (cite omitted). These holdings were, the Court of Appeals reasoned, based on the view that *Miranda* announced a prophylactic rule, a position that it found to be incompatible with this Court's decision in *Dickerson* (cite omitted) ("*Miranda* announced a constitutional rule that Congress may not supersede legislatively"). The Court of Appeals thus equated *Dickerson*'s announcement that *Miranda* is a constitutional rule with the proposition that a failure to warn pursuant to *Miranda* is itself a violation of the Constitution (and, more particularly, of the suspect's Fifth Amendment rights). Based on its understanding of *Dickerson*, the Court of Appeals rejected the

1. The Government concedes that respondent's answers to subsequent on-the-scene questioning are inadmissible at trial under *Miranda* v. *Arizona,* 384 U.S. 436, 86 S. Ct. 1602 (1966), despite the partial warning and respondent's assertions that he knew his rights.

post-*Dickerson* views of the Third and Fourth Circuits that the fruits doctrine does not apply to *Miranda* violations (cites omitted) It also disagreed with the First Circuit's conclusion that suppression is not generally required in the case of negligent failures to warn (cites omitted) ... explaining that "deterrence is necessary not merely to deter intentional wrongdoing, but also to ensure that officers diligently (non-negligently) protect—and properly are trained to protect—the constitutional rights of citizens," (cite omitted). We granted certiorari (cite omitted).

As we explain below, the *Miranda* rule is a prophylactic employed to protect against violations of the Self–Incrimination Clause. The Self–Incrimination Clause, however, is not implicated by the admission into evidence of the physical fruit of a voluntary statement. Accordingly, there is no justification for extending the *Miranda* rule to this context. And just as the Self–Incrimination Clause primarily focuses on the criminal trial, so too does the *Miranda* rule. The *Miranda* rule is not a code of police conduct, and police do not violate the Constitution (or even the *Miranda* rule, for that matter) by mere failures to warn. For this reason, the exclusionary rule articulated in cases such as *Wong Sun* does not apply. Accordingly, we reverse the judgment of the Court of Appeals and remand the case for further proceedings consistent with this opinion.

II

The Self–Incrimination Clause provides: "No person ... shall be compelled in any criminal case to be a witness against himself." U.S. Const., Amdt. 5. We need not decide here the precise boundaries of the Clause's protection. For present purposes, it suffices to note that the core protection afforded by the Self–Incrimination Clause is a prohibition on compelling a criminal defendant to testify against himself at trial (cites omitted).

To be sure, the Court has recognized and applied several prophylactic rules designed to protect the core privilege against self-incrimination (cite omitted)....

Similarly, in *Miranda*, the Court concluded that the possibility of coercion inherent in custodial interrogations unacceptably raises the risk that a suspect's privilege against self-incrimination might be violated. See *Dickerson*, 530 U.S., at 434–435, 120 S. Ct. 2326; *Miranda*, 384 U.S., at 467, 86 S. Ct. 1602. To protect against this danger, the *Miranda* rule creates a presumption of coercion, in the absence of specific warnings, that is generally irrebuttable for purposes of the prosecution's case in chief.

But because these prophylactic rules (including the *Miranda* rule) necessarily sweep beyond the actual protections of the Self–Incrimination Clause, (cites omitted)....

It is for these reasons that statements taken without *Miranda* warnings (though not actually compelled) can be used to impeach a defendant's testimony at trial, (cites omitted). More generally, the *Miranda* rule "does not require that the statements [taken without complying with the rule] and their fruits be discarded as inherently tainted," *Elstad*, 470 U.S., at 307, 105 S. Ct. 1285. Such a blanket suppression rule could not be justified by reference to the "Fifth Amendment goal of assuring trustworthy evidence" or by any deterrence rationale, (cites omitted) and would therefore fail our close-fit requirement.

Furthermore, the Self–Incrimination Clause contains its own exclusionary rule. It provides that "no person ... shall be compelled in any criminal case to be a witness against himself." Amdt. 5. Unlike the Fourth Amendment's bar on unreasonable searches, the Self–Incrimination Clause is self-executing. We have repeatedly explained "that those subjected to coercive police interrogations have an *automatic* protection from the use of their involuntary statements (or evidence derived from their statements) in any subsequent criminal trial." *Chavez*, 538 U.S., at 769, 123 S. Ct. 1994 (plurality opinion) (citing, for example, *Elstad, supra*, at 307–308, 105 S. Ct. 1285). This explicit textual protection supports a strong presumption against expanding the *Miranda* rule any further. Cf. *Graham* v. *Connor,* 490 U.S. 386, 109 S. Ct. 1865 (1989).

Finally, nothing in *Dickerson*, including its characterization of *Miranda* as announcing a constitutional rule, 530 U.S., at 444, 120 S. Ct. 2326, changes any of these observations. Indeed, in *Dickerson*, the Court specifically noted that the Court's "subsequent cases have reduced the impact of the *Miranda* rule on legitimate law enforcement while reaffirming [*Miranda*]'s core ruling that unwarned statements may not be used as evidence in the prosecution's case in chief." *Id.*, at 443–444, 120 S. Ct. 2326. This description of *Miranda*, especially the emphasis on the use of "unwarned statements ... in the prosecution's case in chief," makes clear our continued focus on the protections of the Self–Incrimination Clause. The Court's reliance on our *Miranda* precedents, including both *Tucker* and *Elstad*, see, *e.g., Dickerson*, *supra*, at 438, 441, 147 L. Ed. 2d 405, 120 S. Ct. 2326, further demonstrates the continuing validity of those decisions. In short, nothing in *Dickerson* calls into question our continued insistence that the closest possible fit be maintained between the Self–Incrimination Clause and any rule designed to protect it.

III

Our cases also make clear the related point that a mere failure to give *Miranda* warnings does not, by itself, violate a suspect's constitutional rights or even the *Miranda* rule. So much was evident in many of our pre-*Dickerson* cases, and we have adhered to this view since *Dickerson* (cites omitted)....

It follows that police do not violate a suspect's constitutional rights (or the *Miranda* rule) by negligent or even deliberate failures to provide the suspect with the full panoply of warnings prescribed by *Miranda*. Potential violations occur, if at all, only upon the admission of unwarned statements into evidence at trial. And, at that point, "the exclusion of unwarned statements ... is a complete and sufficient remedy" for any perceived *Miranda* violation (cite omitted).

Thus, unlike unreasonable searches under the Fourth Amendment or actual violations of the Due Process Clause or the Self–Incrimination Clause, there is, with respect to mere failures to warn, nothing to deter. There is therefore no reason to apply the "fruit of the poisonous tree" doctrine of *Wong Sun,* (cite omitted) It is not for this Court to impose its preferred police practices on either federal law enforcement officials or their state counterparts.

IV

In the present case, the Court of Appeals, relying on *Dickerson*, wholly adopted the position that the taking of unwarned statements violates a suspect's constitutional rights (cite omitted). And, of course, if this were so, a strong deterrence-based argument could be made for suppression of the fruits (cites omitted).

But *Dickerson*'s characterization of *Miranda* as a constitutional rule does not lessen the need to maintain the closest possible fit between the Self–Incrimination Clause and any judge-made rule designed to protect it. And there is no such fit here. Introduction of the nontestimonial fruit of a voluntary statement, such as respondent's Glock, does not implicate the Self Incrimination Clause. The admission of such fruit presents no risk that a defendant's coerced statements (however defined) will be used against him at a criminal trial. In any case, "the exclusion of unwarned statements . . . is a complete and sufficient remedy" for any perceived *Miranda* violation. *Chavez*, 538 U.S., at 790, 123 S. Ct. 1994 (Kennedy, J., concurring in part and dissenting in part). See also H. Friendly, Benchmarks 280–281 (1967). There is simply no need to extend (and therefore no justification for extending) the prophylactic rule of *Miranda* to this context.

Similarly, because police cannot violate the Self–Incrimination Clause by taking unwarned though voluntary statements, an exclusionary rule cannot be justified by reference to a deterrence effect on law enforcement, as the Court of Appeals believed (cite omitted), our decision not to apply *Wong Sun* to mere failures to give *Miranda* warnings was sound at the time *Tucker* and *Elstad* were decided, and we decline to apply *Wong Sun* to such failures now. . . .

Accordingly, we reverse the judgment of the Court of Appeals and remand the case for further proceedings consistent with this opinion.

It is so ordered.

■ CONCUR: JUSTICE KENNEDY, with whom JUSTICE O'CONNOR joins, concurring in the judgment

In *Oregon* v. *Elstad*, *New York* v. *Quarles*, and *Harris* v. *New York* (cites omitted), evidence obtained following an unwarned interrogation was held admissible. This result was based in large part on our recognition that the concerns underlying the *Miranda* v. *Arizona,* 384 U.S. 436, 86 S. Ct. 1602 (1966), rule must be accommodated to other objectives of the criminal justice system. I agree with the plurality that *Dickerson* v. *United States*, 530 U.S. 428, 120 S. Ct. 2326 (2000), did not undermine these precedents and, in fact, cited them in support. Here, it is sufficient to note that the Government presents an even stronger case for admitting the evidence obtained as the result of Patane's unwarned statement. Admission of nontestimonial physical fruits (the Glock in this case), even more so than the postwarning statements to the police in *Elstad* and *Michigan* v. *Tucker*, 417 U.S. 433, 94 S. Ct. 2357 (1974), does not run the risk of admitting into trial an accused's coerced incriminating statements against himself. In light of the important probative value of reliable physical evidence, it is doubtful that exclusion can be justified by a deterrence rationale sensitive to both law enforcement interests and a suspect's rights during an in-custody interrogation. Unlike the plurality, however, I find it unnecessary to decide whether the detective's failure to give Patane the full *Miranda* warnings should be characterized as a violation of the *Miranda* rule itself, or whether there is "anything to deter" so long as the unwarned statements are not later introduced at trial.

With these observations, I concur in the judgment of the Court.

■ DISSENT: JUSTICE SOUTER, with whom JUSTICE STEVENS and JUSTICE GINSBURG join, dissenting.

The majority repeatedly says that the Fifth Amendment does not address the admissibility of nontestimonial evidence, an overstatement that is beside the point. The issue actually presented today is whether courts should apply the fruit of the poisonous tree doctrine lest we create an incentive for the police to omit *Miranda* warnings, see *Miranda* v. *Arizona*, 384 U.S. 436, 86 S. Ct. 1602 (1966), before custodial interrogation.[1] In closing their eyes to the consequences of giving an evidentiary advantage to those who ignore *Miranda*, the majority adds an important inducement for interrogators to ignore the rule in that case.

Miranda rested on insight into the inherently coercive character of custodial interrogation and the inherently difficult exercise of assessing the voluntariness of any confession resulting from it. Unless the police give the prescribed warnings meant to counter the coercive atmosphere, a custodial confession is inadmissible, there being no need for the previous time-consuming and difficult enquiry into voluntariness. That inducement to forestall involuntary statements and troublesome issues of fact can only atrophy if we turn around and recognize an evidentiary benefit when an unwarned statement leads investigators to tangible evidence. There is, of course, a price for excluding evidence, but the Fifth Amendment is worth a price, and in the absence of a very good reason, the logic of *Miranda* should be followed: a *Miranda* violation raises a presumption of coercion, *Oregon v. Elstad*, 470 U.S. 298, 306–307, 105 S. Ct. 1285, and the Fifth Amendment privilege against compelled self-incrimination extends to the exclusion of derivative evidence, see *United States* v. *Hubbell*, 530 U.S. 27, 37–38, 120 S. Ct. 2037 (2000) (recognizing "the Fifth Amendment's protection against the prosecutor's use of incriminating information derived directly or indirectly from . . . [actually] compelled testimony"); *Kastigar* v. *United States*, 406 U.S. 441, 453, 92 S. Ct. 1653 (1972). That should be the end of this case.

The fact that the books contain some exceptions to the *Miranda* exclusionary rule carries no weight here. In *Harris* v. *New York*, 401 U.S.

1. In so saying, we are taking the legal issue as it comes to us, even though the facts give off the scent of a made-up case. If there was a *Miranda* failure, the most immediate reason was that Patane told the police to stop giving the warnings because he already knew his rights. There could easily be an analogy in this case to the bumbling mistake the police committed in *Oregon* v. *Elstad*, 470 U.S. 298, 105 S. Ct. 1285 (1985). See *Missouri* v. *Seibert*, ___ U.S. ___, 124 S. Ct. 2601 (2004) (plurality opinion).

222, 91 S. Ct. 643 (1971), it was respect for the integrity of the judicial process that justified the admission of unwarned statements as impeachment evidence. But Patane's suppression motion can hardly be described as seeking to "pervert" *Miranda* "into a license to use perjury" or otherwise handicap the "traditional truth-testing devices of the adversary process" (cite omitted). Nor is there any suggestion that the officers' failure to warn Patane was justified or mitigated by a public emergency or other exigent circumstance, as in *New York* v. *Quarles*, 467 U.S. 649, 104 S. Ct. 2626 (1984). And of course the premise of *Oregon* v. *Elstad*, *supra*, is not on point; although a failure to give *Miranda* warnings before one individual statement does not necessarily bar the admission of a subsequent statement given after adequate warnings, 470 U.S. 298, 105 S. Ct. 1285; cf. *Missouri* v. *Seibert* (cite omitted) (plurality opinion), that rule obviously does not apply to physical evidence seized once and for all. [2]

There is no way to read this case except as an unjustifiable invitation to law enforcement officers to flout *Miranda* when there may be physical evidence to be gained. The incentive is an odd one, coming from the Court on the same day it decides *Missouri* v. *Seibert*. I respectfully dissent.

■ JUSTICE BREYER, dissenting.

For reasons similar to those set forth in JUSTICE SOUTER'S dissent and in my concurring opinion in *Missouri* v. *Seibert*, I would extend to this context the "fruit of the poisonous tree" approach, which I believe the Court has come close to adopting in *Seibert*. Under that approach, courts would exclude physical evidence derived from unwarned questioning unless the failure to provide *Miranda* warnings was in good faith (cites omitted). Because the courts below made no explicit finding as to good or bad faith, I would remand for such a determination.

G. DERIVATIVE EVIDENCE: PRINCIPLES AND LIMITATIONS

Add at end of note 7 on pages 668–669:

Does *Elstad* apply when the Sixth Amendment has attached?

John J. Fellers v. United States

___ U.S. ___, 124 S.Ct. 1019 (January 26, 2004).

■ OPINION: JUSTICE O'CONNOR delivered the opinion of the Court.

After a grand jury indicted petitioner John J. Fellers, police officers arrested him at his home. During the course of the arrest, petitioner made

2. To the extent that *Michigan* v. *Tucker*, 417 U.S. 433, 94 S. Ct. 2357 (1974) (admitting the testimony of a witness who was discovered because of an unwarned custodial interrogation), created another exception to *Miranda*, it is off the point here. In *Tucker*, we explicitly declined to lay down a broad rule about the fruits of unwarned statements. Instead, we "placed our holding on a narrower ground," relying principally on the fact that the interrogation occurred before *Miranda* was decided and was conducted in good faith according to constitutional standards governing at that time. 417 U.S., at 447–448, 94 S. Ct. 2357 (citing *Escobedo v. Illinois*, 378 U.S. 478, 84 S. Ct. 1758 (1964)).

several inculpatory statements. He argued that the officers deliberately elicited these statements from him outside the presence of counsel, and that the admission at trial of the fruits of those statements therefore violated his Sixth Amendment right to counsel. Petitioner contends that in rejecting this argument, the Court of Appeals for the Eighth Circuit improperly held that the Sixth Amendment right to counsel was "not applicable" because "the officers did not interrogate [petitioner] at his home." We granted the petition for a writ of certiorari, (cites omitted), and now reverse.

I

On February 24, 2000, after a grand jury indicted petitioner for conspiracy to distribute methamphetamine, Lincoln Police Sergeant Michael Garnett and Lancaster County Deputy Sheriff Jeff Bliemeister went to petitioner's home in Lincoln, Nebraska, to arrest him. The officers knocked on petitioner's door and, when petitioner answered, identified themselves and asked if they could come in. Petitioner invited the officers into his living room (cites omitted).

The officers advised petitioner they had come to discuss his involvement in methamphetamine distribution. They informed petitioner that they had a federal warrant for his arrest and that a grand jury had indicted him for conspiracy to distribute methamphetamine. The officers told petitioner that the indictment referred to his involvement with certain individuals, four of whom they named. Petitioner then told the officers that he knew the four people and had used methamphetamine during his association with them.

After spending about 15 minutes in petitioner's home, the officers transported petitioner to the Lancaster County jail. There, the officers advised petitioner for the first time of his rights under *Miranda* v. Arizona, and *Patterson* v. *Illinois,* (cites omitted) Petitioner and the two officers signed a *Miranda* waiver form, and petitioner then reiterated the inculpatory statements he had made earlier, admitted to having associated with other individuals implicated in the charged conspiracy, and admitted to having loaned money to one of them even though he suspected that she was involved in drug transactions.

Before trial, petitioner moved to suppress the inculpatory statements he made at his home and at the county jail. A Magistrate Judge conducted a hearing and recommended that the statements petitioner made at his home be suppressed because the officers had not informed petitioner of his *Miranda* rights. The Magistrate Judge found that petitioner made the statements in response to the officers' "implici[t] questions," noting that the officers had told petitioner that the purpose of their visit was to discuss his use and distribution of methamphetamine. The Magistrate Judge further recommended that portions of petitioner's jailhouse statement be suppressed as fruits of the prior failure to provide *Miranda* warnings.

The District Court suppressed the "unwarned" statements petitioner made at his house but admitted petitioner's jailhouse statements pursuant to *Oregon* v. *Elstad,* (cite omitted), concluding petitioner had knowingly and voluntarily waived his *Miranda* rights before making the statements.

Following a jury trial at which petitioner's jailhouse statements were admitted into evidence, petitioner was convicted of conspiring to possess with intent to distribute methamphetamine. Petitioner appealed, arguing that his jailhouse statements should have been suppressed as fruits of the statements obtained at his home in violation of the Sixth Amendment. The Court of Appeals affirmed (cite omitted). With respect to petitioner's argument that the officers' failure to administer *Miranda* warnings at his home violated his Sixth Amendment right to counsel under *Patterson, supra*, the Court of Appeals stated: "*Patterson* is not applicable here . . . for the officers did not interrogate [petitioner] at his home." The Court of Appeals also concluded that the statements from the jail were properly admitted under the rule of *Elstad* (" 'Though *Miranda* requires that the unwarned admission must be suppressed, the admissibility of any subsequent statement should turn in these circumstances solely on whether it is knowingly and voluntarily made' " (quoting *Elstad, supra*, at 309, 84 L. Ed. 2d 222, 105 S. Ct. 1285)).

Judge Riley filed a concurring opinion. He concluded that during their conversation at petitioner's home, officers "deliberately elicited incriminating information" from petitioner (cite omitted). That "post-indictment conduct outside the presence of counsel," Judge Riley reasoned, violated petitioner's Sixth Amendment rights. Judge Riley nevertheless concurred in the judgment, concluding that the jailhouse statements were admissible under the rationale of *Elstad* in light of petitioner's knowing and voluntary waiver of his right to counsel.

II

The Sixth Amendment right to counsel is triggered "at or after the time that judicial proceedings have been initiated . . . 'whether by way of formal charge, preliminary hearing, indictment, information, or arraignment.' " *Brewer* v. *Williams,* 430 U.S. 387, 398, 97 S. Ct. 1232 (1977) (quoting *Kirby* v. *Illinois,* 406 U.S. 682, 689, 92 S. Ct. 1877 (1972)). We have held that an accused is denied "the basic protections" of the Sixth Amendment "when there [is] used against him at his trial evidence of his own incriminating words, which federal agents . . . deliberately elicited from him after he had been indicted and in the absence of his counsel." *Massiah* v. *United States,* 377 U.S. 201, 206, 84 S. Ct. 1199 (1964); cf. *Patterson* v. *Illinois, supra* (holding that the Sixth Amendment does not bar postindictment questioning in the absence of counsel if a defendant waives the right to counsel).

We have consistently applied the deliberate-elicitation standard in subsequent Sixth Amendment cases, see *United States v. Henry,* (cite omitted)("The question here is whether under the facts of this case a Government agent 'deliberately elicited' incriminating statements . . . within the meaning of *Massiah*"); *Brewer, supra,* at 399, 97 S. Ct. 1232 (finding a Sixth Amendment violation where a detective "deliberately and designedly set out to elicit information from [the suspect]"), and we have expressly distinguished this standard from the Fifth Amendment custodial-interrogation standard, see *Michigan* v. *Jackson,* 475 U.S. 625, 632, n. 5, 106 S. Ct. 1404 (1986) ("[T]he Sixth Amendment provides a right to counsel . . . even when there is no interrogation and no Fifth Amendment applicability''); *Rhode Island* v. *Innis,* 446 U.S. 291, 300, n. 4, 100 S. Ct. 1682 (1980) (''The definitions of 'interrogation' under the Fifth and Sixth Amendments, if indeed the term 'interrogation' is even apt in the Sixth Amendment context, are not necessarily interchangeable''); cf. *United States* v. *Wade,* 388 U.S. 218, 87 S. Ct. 1926 (1967) (holding that the Sixth Amendment provides the right to counsel at a postindictment lineup even though the Fifth Amendment is not implicated).

The Court of Appeals erred in holding that the absence of an ''interrogation'' foreclosed petitioner's claim that the jailhouse statements should have been suppressed as fruits of the statements taken from petitioner at his home. First, there is no question that the officers in this case ''deliberately elicited'' information from petitioner. Indeed, the officers, upon arriving at petitioner's house, informed him that their purpose in coming was to discuss his involvement in the distribution of methamphetamine and his association with certain charged co-conspirators (cite omitted). Because the ensuing discussion took place after petitioner had been indicted, outside the presence of counsel, and in the absence of any waiver of petitioner's Sixth Amendment rights, the Court of Appeals erred in holding that the officers' actions did not violate the Sixth Amendment standards established in *Massiah, supra*, and its progeny.

Second, because of its erroneous determination that petitioner was not questioned in violation of Sixth Amendment standards, the Court of Appeals improperly conducted its ''fruits'' analysis under the Fifth Amendment. Specifically, it applied *Elstad, supra*, to hold that the admissibility of the jailhouse statements turns solely on whether the statements were '' 'knowingly and voluntarily made' '' (cites omitted). The Court of Appeals did not reach the question whether the Sixth Amendment requires suppression of petitioner's jailhouse statements on the ground that they were the fruits of previous questioning conducted in violation of the Sixth Amendment deliberate-elicitation standard. We have not had occasion to decide whether the rationale of *Elstad* applies when a suspect makes incriminating statements after a knowing and voluntary waiver of his right to counsel notwithstanding earlier police questioning in violation of Sixth Amendment standards. We therefore remand to the Court of Appeals to address this issue in the first instance.

Accordingly, the judgment of the Court of Appeals is reversed, and the case is remanded for further proceedings consistent with this opinion.

* * *

Add after note 7 on page 669:

The Supreme Court revisited the validity of the ''question first'' tactics permitted by *Elstad* in the following case:

Missouri v. Seibert

___ U.S. ___, 124 S.Ct. 2601 (June 28, 2004).

■ OPINION: JUSTICE SOUTER announced the judgment of the Court and delivered an opinion, in which JUSTICE STEVENS, JUSTICE GINSBURG, and JUSTICE BREYER join.

This case tests a police protocol for custodial interrogation that calls for giving no warnings of the rights to silence and counsel until interrogation has produced a confession. Although such a statement is generally inadmissible, since taken in violation of *Miranda* v. *Arizona*, 384 U.S. 436, 86 S. Ct. 1602 (1966), the interrogating officer follows it with *Miranda* warnings and then leads the suspect to cover the same ground a second time. The question here is the admissibility of the repeated statement. Because this midstream recitation of warnings after interrogation and unwarned confession could not effectively comply with *Miranda*'s constitutional requirement, we hold that a statement repeated after a warning in such circumstances is inadmissible.

I

Respondent Patrice Seibert's 12–year-old son Jonathan had cerebral palsy, and when he died in his sleep she feared charges of neglect because of bedsores on his body. In her presence, two of her teenage sons and two of their friends devised a plan to conceal the facts surrounding Jonathan's death by incinerating his body in the course of burning the family's mobile home, in which they planned to leave Donald Rector, a mentally ill teenager living with the family, to avoid any appearance that Jonathan had been unattended. Seibert's son Darian and a friend set the fire, and Donald died.

Five days later, the police awakened Seibert at 3 a.m. at a hospital where Darian was being treated for burns. In arresting her, Officer Kevin Clinton followed instructions from Rolla, Missouri, officer Richard Hanrahan that he refrain from giving *Miranda* warnings. After Seibert had been taken to the police station and left alone in an interview room for 15 to 20 minutes, Hanrahan questioned her without *Miranda* warnings for 30 to 40 minutes, squeezing her arm and repeating "Donald was also to die in his sleep." App. 59 (internal quotation marks omitted). After Seibert finally admitted she knew Donald was meant to die in the fire, she was given a 20–minute coffee and cigarette break. Officer Hanrahan then turned on a tape recorder, gave Seibert the *Miranda* warnings, and obtained a signed waiver of rights from her. He resumed the questioning with "Ok, 'trice, we've been talking for a little while about what happened on Wednesday the twelfth, haven't we?," App. 66, and confronted her with her prewarning statements:

Hanrahan: "Now, in discussion you told us, you told us that there was an understanding about Donald."

Seibert: "Yes."

Hanrahan: "Did that take place earlier that morning?"

Seibert: "Yes."

Hanrahan: "And what was the understanding about Donald?"

Seibert: "If they could get him out of the trailer, to take him out of the trailer."

Hanrahan: "And if they couldn't?"

Seibert: "I, I never even thought about it. I just figured they would."

Hanrahan: " 'Trice, didn't you tell me that he was supposed to die in his sleep?' "

Seibert: "If that would happen, 'cause he was on that new medicine, you know...."

Hanrahan: "The Prozac? And it makes him sleepy. So he was supposed to die in his sleep?"

Seibert: "Yes." *Id.*, at 70.

After being charged with first-degree murder for her role in Donald's death, Seibert sought to exclude both her prewarning and postwarning statements. At the suppression hearing, Officer Hanrahan testified that he made a "conscious decision" to withhold *Miranda* warnings, thus resorting to an interrogation technique he had been taught: question first, then give the warnings, and then repeat the question "until I get the answer that she's already provided once." App. 31–34. He acknowledged that Seibert's ultimate statement was "largely a repeat of information ... obtained" prior to the warning. *Id.*, at 30.

The trial court suppressed the prewarning statement but admitted the responses given after the *Miranda* recitation. A jury convicted Seibert of second-degree murder. On appeal, the Missouri Court of Appeals affirmed, treating this case as indistinguishable from *Oregon v. Elstad*, 470 U.S. 298, 105 S. Ct. 1285 (1985).

The Supreme Court of Missouri reversed, holding that "in the circumstances here, where the interrogation was nearly continuous, ... the second statement, clearly the product of the invalid first statement, should have been suppressed" (cite omitted). The court distinguished *Elstad* on the ground that warnings had not intentionally been withheld there, (cite omitted), and reasoned that "Officer Hanrahan's intentional omission of a *Miranda* warning was intended to deprive Seibert of the opportunity knowingly and intelligently to waive her *Miranda* rights," (cite omitted). Since there were "no circumstances that would seem to dispel the effect of the *Miranda* violation," the court held that the postwarning confession was involuntary and therefore inadmissible. *Ibid.* To allow the police to achieve an "end run" around *Miranda*, the court explained, would encourage *Miranda* violations and diminish *Miranda*'s role in protecting the privilege against self-incrimination (cite omitted). One judge dissented, taking the view that *Elstad* applied even though the police intentionally withheld *Miranda* warnings before the initial statement, and believing that "Seibert's unwarned responses to Officer Hanrahan's questioning did not prevent her from waiving her rights and confessing." 93 S. W. 3d, at 708 (opinion of Benton, J.).

We granted certiorari to resolve a split in the Courts of Appeals.... We now affirm.

II

"In criminal trials, in the courts of the United States, wherever a question arises whether a confession is incompetent because not voluntary, the issue is controlled by that portion of the Fifth Amendment ... commanding that no person 'shall be compelled in any criminal case to be a witness against himself.' " *Bram* v. *United States*, 168 U.S. 532, 542, 18 S. Ct. 183 (1897). A parallel rule governing the admissibility of confessions in state courts emerged from the Due Process Clause of the Fourteenth Amendment, see, *e.g.*, *Brown* v. *Mississippi*, 297 U.S. 278, 80 L. Ed. 682, 56 S. Ct. 461 (1936), which governed state cases until we concluded in *Malloy* v. *Hogan*, 378 U.S. 1, 8, 84 S. Ct. 1489 (1964), that "the Fourteenth Amendment secures against state invasion the same privilege that the Fifth Amendment guarantees against federal infringement—the right of a person to remain silent unless he chooses to speak in the unfettered exercise of his own will, and to suffer no penalty ... for such silence." "In unifying the Fifth and Fourteenth Amendment voluntariness tests, *Malloy* 'made clear what had already become apparent—that the substantive and procedural safeguards surrounding admissibility of confessions in state cases had become exceedingly exacting, reflecting all the policies embedded in the privilege' against self-incrimination." *Miranda*, 384 U.S., at 464, 86 S. Ct. 1602 .

In *Miranda*, we explained that the "voluntariness doctrine in the state cases ... encompasses all interrogation practices which are likely to exert such pressure upon an individual as to disable him from making a free and rational choice," (cite omitted). We appreciated the difficulty of judicial enquiry *post hoc* into the circumstances of a police interrogation, *Dickerson v. United States* (cite omitted), and recognized that "the coercion inherent in custodial interrogation blurs the line between voluntary and involuntary statements, and thus heightens the risk" that the privilege against self-incrimination will not be observed, (cite omitted). Hence our concern that the "traditional totality-of-the-circumstances" test posed an "unacceptably great" risk that involuntary custodial confessions would escape detection (cite omitted).

Accordingly, "to reduce the risk of a coerced confession and to implement the Self–Incrimination Clause," (cite omitted) this Court in *Miranda* concluded that "the accused must be adequately and effectively apprised of his rights and the exercise of those rights must be fully honored," (cite omitted).

Miranda conditioned the admissibility at trial of any custodial confession on warning a suspect of his rights: failure to give the prescribed warnings and obtain a waiver of rights before custodial questioning generally requires exclusion of any statements obtained. Conversely, giving the warnings and getting a waiver has generally produced a virtual ticket of admissibility; maintaining that a statement is involuntary even though given after warnings and voluntary waiver of rights requires unusual stamina, and litigation over voluntariness tends to end with the finding of a valid waiver. See *Berkemer* v. *McCarty*, 468 U.S. 420, 433, n. 20, 104 S. Ct. 3138 (1984) ("Cases in which a defendant can make a colorable argument that a self-incriminating statement was 'compelled' despite the fact that the law enforcement authorities adhered to the dictates of *Miranda* are rare"). To point out the obvious, this common consequence would not be common at all were it not that *Miranda* warnings are customarily given under circumstances allowing for a real choice between talking and remaining silent.

III

There are those, of course, who preferred the old way of doing things, giving no warnings and litigating the voluntariness of any statement in nearly every instance. In the aftermath of *Miranda*, Congress even passed a statute seeking to restore that old regime, 18 U.S.C. § 3501, although the Act lay dormant for years until finally invoked and challenged in *Dickerson* v. *United States*.... *Dickerson* reaffirmed *Miranda* and held that its constitutional character prevailed against the statute.

The technique of interrogating in successive, unwarned and warned phases raises a new challenge to *Miranda*. Although we have no statistics on the frequency of this practice, it is not confined to Rolla, Missouri. An officer of that police department testified that the strategy of withholding *Miranda* warnings until after interrogating and drawing out a confession was promoted not only by his own department, but by a national police training organization and other departments in which he had worked. App. 31–32. Consistently with the officer's testimony, the Police Law Institute, for example, instructs that "officers may conduct a two-stage interrogation.... At any point during the pre-*Miranda* interrogation, usually after arrestees have confessed, officers may then read the *Miranda* warnings and ask for a waiver. If the arrestees waive their *Miranda* rights, officers will be able to repeat any *subsequent* incriminating statements later in court." Police Law Institute, Illinois Police Law Manual 83 (Jan. 2001–Dec. 2003), http://www.illinoispolicelaw.org/training/lessons/ ILPLMIR.pdf (as visited Dec. 31, 2003, and available in the Clerk of Court's case file) (hereinafter Police Law Manual) (emphasis in original).[3] The upshot of all this advice is a question-first practice of some popularity, as one can see from the

3. Emphasizing the impeachment exception to the *Miranda* rule approved by this Court, *Harris* v. *New York*, 401 U.S. 222, 91 S. Ct. 643 (1971), some training programs advise officers to omit *Miranda* warnings altogether or to continue questioning after the suspect invokes his rights. See, *e.g.*, Police Law Manual 83 ("There is no need to give a *Miranda* warning before asking questions if ... the answers given ... will not be required by the prosecutor during the prosecution's case-in-chief"); California Commission on Peace Officer Standards and Training, Video Training Programs for California Law Enforcement, Miranda: Post–Invocation Questioning (broadcast July 11, 1996) ("We ... have been encouraging you to continue to question a suspect after they've invoked their *Miranda* rights"); D. Zulawski & D. Wicklander, Practical Aspects of Interview and Interrogation 50–51 (2d ed. 2002) (describing the practice of "beachheading" as useful for impeachment purpose (emphasis deleted)); see also Weisselberg, Saving *Miranda,* 84 Cornell L. Rev. 109, 110, 132–139 (1998) (collecting California training materials encouraging questioning "outside *Miranda*"). This training is reflected in the reported cases involving deliberate questioning after invocation of *Miranda* rights (cites omitted). Scholars have noted the growing trend of such practices. See, *e.g.*, Leo, Questioning the Relevance of *Miranda* in the Twenty–First Century, 99 Mich. L. Rev. 1000, 1010 (2001); Weisselberg, In the Stationhouse After *Dickerson*, 99 Mich. L. Rev. 1121, 1123–1154 (2001).

It is not the case, of course, that law enforcement educators en masse are urging that *Miranda* be honored only in the breach (cites omitted).... Most police manuals do not advocate the question-first tactic, because they understand that *Oregon v. Elstad* (cite omitted), involved an officer's good-faith failure to warn. See, *e.g.*, Inbau, Reid, & Buckley 241 (*Elstad*'s "facts as well as [its] specific holding" instruct that "where an interrogator has failed to administer the *Miranda* warnings in the mistaken belief that, under the circumstances of the particular case, the warnings were not required, ... corrective measures ... salvage an interrogation opportunity").

reported cases describing its use, sometimes in obedience to departmental policy.

IV

When a confession so obtained is offered and challenged, attention must be paid to the conflicting objects of *Miranda* and question-first. *Miranda* addressed "interrogation practices ... likely ... to disable [an individual] from making a free and rational choice" about speaking, 384 U.S., at 464–465, 86 S. Ct. 1602, and held that a suspect must be "adequately and effectively" advised of the choice the Constitution guarantees, id., at 467, 86 S. Ct. 1602. The object of question-first is to render *Miranda* warnings ineffective by waiting for a particularly opportune time to give them, after the suspect has already confessed.

Just as "no talismanic incantation [is] required to satisfy [*Miranda*'s] strictures," (cite omitted) it would be absurd to think that mere recitation of the litany suffices to satisfy *Miranda* in every conceivable circumstance. "The inquiry is simply whether the warnings reasonably 'convey to [a suspect] his rights as required by *Miranda*.'" *Duckworth* v. *Eagan*, 492 U.S. 195, 203, 109 S. Ct. 2875 (1989) (quoting *Prysock*, *supra*, at 361, 101 S. Ct. 2806). The threshold issue when interrogators question first and warn later is thus whether it would be reasonable to find that in these circumstances the warnings could function "effectively" as *Miranda* requires. Could the warnings effectively advise the suspect that he had a real choice about giving an admissible statement at that juncture? Could they reasonably convey that he could choose to stop talking even if he had talked earlier? For unless the warnings could place a suspect who has just been interrogated in practical justification for accepting the formal warnings as compliance with *Miranda*, or for treating the second stage of interrogation as distinct from the first, unwarned and inadmissible segment.[4]

4. Respondent Seibert argues that her second confession should be excluded from evidence under the doctrine known by the metaphor of the "fruit of the poisonous tree," developed in the Fourth Amendment context in *Wong Sun* v. *United States*, 371 U.S. 471, 83 S. Ct. 407 (1963): evidence otherwise admissible but discovered as a result of an earlier violation is excluded as tainted, lest the law encourage future violations. But the Court in *Elstad* rejected the *Wong Sun* fruits doctrine for analyzing the admissibility of a subsequent warned confession following "an initial failure ... to administer the warnings required by *Miranda*." *Elstad*, 470 U.S., at 300, 105 S. Ct. 1285. In *Elstad*, "a simple failure to administer the warnings, unaccompanied by any actual coercion or other circumstances calculated to undermine the suspect's ability to exercise his free will" did not "so taint the investigatory process that a subsequent voluntary and informed waiver is ineffective for some indeterminate period. Though *Miranda* requires that the unwarned admission must be suppressed, the admissibility of any subsequent statement should turn in these circumstances solely on whether it is knowingly and voluntarily made" (cite omitted) . *Elstad* held that "a suspect who has once responded to unwarned yet uncoercive questioning is not thereby disabled from waiving his rights and confessing after he has been given the requisite *Miranda* warnings." (cite omitted). In a sequential confession case, clarity is served if the later confession is approached by asking whether in the circumstances the *Miranda* warnings given could reasonably be found effective. If yes, a court can take up the standard issues of voluntary waiver and voluntary statement; if no, the subsequent statement is inadmissible for want of adequate *Miranda* warnings, because the earlier and later statements are realistically seen as parts of a single, unwarned sequence of questioning.

There is no doubt about the answer that proponents of question-first give to this question about the effectiveness of warnings given only after successful interrogation, and we think their answer is correct. By any objective measure, applied to circumstances exemplified here, it is likely that if the interrogators employ the technique of withholding warnings until after interrogation succeeds in eliciting a confession, the warnings will be ineffective in preparing the suspect for successive interrogation, close in time and similar in content. After all, the reason that question-first is catching on is as obvious as its manifest purpose, which is to get a confession the suspect would not make if he understood his rights at the outset; the sensible underlying assumption is that with one confession in hand before the warnings, the interrogator can count on getting its duplicate, with trifling additional trouble. Upon hearing warnings only in the aftermath of interrogation and just after making a confession, a suspect would hardly think he had a genuine right to remain silent, let alone persist in so believing once the police began to lead him over the same ground again.[5] A more likely reaction on a suspect's part would be perplexity about the reason for discussing rights at that point, bewilderment being an unpromising frame of mind for knowledgeable decision. What is worse, telling a suspect that "anything you say can and will be used against you," without expressly excepting the statement just given, could lead to an entirely reasonable inference that what he has just said will be used, with subsequent silence being of no avail. Thus,."when *Miranda* warnings are inserted in the midst of coordinated and continuing interrogation, they are likely to mislead and 'deprive a defendant of knowledge essential to his ability to understand the nature of his rights and the consequences of abandoning them.' " *Moran* v. *Burbine*, 475 U.S. 412, 424, 106 S. Ct. 1135 (1986). By the same token, it would ordinarily be unrealistic to treat two spates of integrated and proximately conducted questioning as independent interrogations subject to independent evaluation simply because *Miranda* warnings formally punctuate them in the middle.

V

Missouri argues that a confession repeated at the end of an interrogation sequence envisioned in a question-first strategy is admissible on the authority of *Oregon* v. *Elstad*, 470 U.S. 298, 105 S. Ct. 1285 (1985), but the argument disfigures that case. In *Elstad*, the police went to the young suspect's house to take him into custody on a charge of burglary. Before the arrest, one officer spoke with the suspect's mother, while the other one joined the suspect in a "brief stop in the living room," where the officer said he "felt" the young man was involved in a burglary, (internal quotation marks omitted). The suspect acknowledged he had been at the scene. This Court noted that the pause in the living room "was not to interrogate

5. It bears emphasizing that the effectiveness *Miranda* assumes the warnings can have must potentially extend through the repeated interrogation, since a suspect has a right to stop at any time. It seems highly unlikely that a suspect could retain any such understanding when the interrogator leads him a second time through a line of questioning the suspect has already answered fully. The point is not that a later unknowing or involuntary confession cancels out an earlier, adequate warning; the point is that the warning is unlikely to be effective in the question-first sequence we have described.

the suspect but to notify his mother of the reason for his arrest,'', and described the incident as having "none of the earmarks of coercion. "The Court, indeed, took care to mention that the officer's initial failure to warn was an "oversight" that "may have been the result of confusion as to whether the brief exchange qualified as 'custodial interrogation' or . . . may simply have reflected . . . reluctance to initiate an alarming police procedure before [an officer] had spoken with respondent's mother." At the outset of a later and systematic station house interrogation going well beyond the scope of the laconic prior admission, the suspect was given *Miranda* warnings and made a full confession. In holding the second statement admissible and voluntary, *Elstad* rejected the "cat out of the bag" theory that any short, earlier admission, obtained in arguably innocent neglect of *Miranda,* determined the character of the later, warned confession; on the facts of that case, the Court thought any causal connection between the first and second responses to the police was "speculative and attenuated.". Although the *Elstad* Court expressed no explicit conclusion about either officer's state of mind, it is fair to read *Elstad* as treating the living room conversation as a good-faith *Miranda* mistake, not only open to correction by careful warnings before systematic questioning in that particular case, but posing no threat to warn-first practice generally. See *Elstad,* (characterizing the officers' omission of *Miranda* warnings as "a simple failure to administer the warnings, unaccompanied by any actual coercion or other circumstances calculated to undermine the suspect's ability to exercise his free will");(Justice Brennan's concern in dissent that *Elstad* would invite question-first practice "distorts the reasoning and holding of our decision, but, worse, invites trial courts and prosecutors to do the same") (citations to *Elstad* omitted).

The contrast between *Elstad* and this case reveals "a series of relevant facts that bear on whether *Miranda* warnings delivered midstream could be effective enough to accomplish their object: the completeness and detail of the questions and answers in the first round of interrogation, the overlapping content of the two statements, the timing and setting of the first and the second, the continuity of police personnel, and the degree to which the interrogator's questions treated the second round as continuous with the first. In *Elstad,* it was not unreasonable to see the occasion for questioning at the station house as presenting a markedly different experience from the short conversation at home; since a reasonable person in the suspect's shoes could have seen the station house questioning as a new and distinct experience, the *Miranda* warnings could have made sense as presenting a genuine choice whether to follow up on the earlier admission.

At the opposite extreme are the facts here, which by any objective measure reveal a police strategy adapted to undermine the *Miranda* warnings. [6]The unwarned interrogation was conducted in the station house, and the questioning was systematic, exhaustive, and managed with psychological skill. When the police were finished there was little, if anything, of incriminating potential left unsaid. The warned phase of questioning pro-

6. Because the intent of the officer will rarely be as candidly admitted as it was here (even as it is likely to determine the conduct of the interrogation), the focus is on facts apart from intent that show the question-first tactic at work ceeded after a pause of only 15 to 20 minutes, in the same place as the unwarned segment. When the same officer who had conducted the first phase recited the *Miranda* warnings, he said nothing to counter the probable misimpression that the advice that anything Seibert said could be used against her also applied to the details of the inculpatory statement previously elicited. In particular, the police did not advise that her prior statement could not be used.[7] Nothing was said or done to dispel the oddity of warning about legal rights to silence and counsel right after the police had led her through a systematic interrogation, and any uncertainty on her part about a right to stop talking about matters previously discussed would only have been aggravated by the way Officer Hanrahan set the scene by saying "we've been talking for a little while about what happened on Wednesday the twelfth, haven't we?" App. 66. The impression that the further questioning was a mere continuation of the earlier questions and responses was fostered by references back to the confession already given. It would have been reasonable to regard the two sessions as parts of a continuum, in which it would have been unnatural to refuse to repeat at the second stage what had been said before. These circumstances must be seen as challenging the comprehensibility and efficacy of the *Miranda* warnings to the point that a reasonable person in the suspect's shoes would not have understood them to convey a message that she retained a choice about continuing to talk.[8]

VI

Strategists dedicated to draining the substance out of *Miranda* cannot accomplish by training instructions what *Dickerson* held Congress could not do by statute. Because the question-first tactic effectively threatens to thwart *Miranda*'s purpose of reducing the risk that a coerced confession would be admitted, and because the facts here do not reasonably support a conclusion that the warnings given could have served their purpose, Seibert's postwarning statements are inadmissible. The judgment of the Supreme Court of Missouri is affirmed.

It is so ordered.

■ CONCUR: JUSTICE BREYER, concurring (with whom Justice Kennedy joins).

In my view, the following simple rule should apply to the two-stage interrogation technique: Courts should exclude the "fruits" of the initial unwarned questioning unless the failure to warn was in good faith. Cf. *Oregon* v. *Elstad*, 470 U.S. 298, 309, 318, n. 5, 105 S. Ct. 1285 (1985); *United States v. Leon*, 468 U.S. 897, 104 S. Ct. 3405 (1984). I believe this is a sound and workable approach to the problem this case presents. Prosecutors and judges have long understood how to apply the "fruits" approach, which they use in other areas of law. See *Wong Sun* v. *United States*, 371

7. We do not hold that a formal addendum warning that a previous statement could not be used would be sufficient to change the character of the question-first procedure to the point of rendering an ensuing statement admissible, but its absence is clearly a factor that blunts the efficacy of the warnings and points to a continuing, not a new, interrogation.

8. Because we find that the warnings were inadequate, there is no need to assess the actual voluntariness of the statement.

U.S. 471, 83 S. Ct. 407 (1963). And in the workaday world of criminal law enforcement the administrative simplicity of the familiar has significant advantages over a more complex exclusionary rule. Cf. *post*, at 6–7 (O'Connor, J., dissenting). . . .

■ JUSTICE KENNEDY, concurring in the judgment.

The interrogation technique used in this case is designed to circumvent *Miranda v. Arizona*, 384 U.S. 436, 86 S. Ct. 1602 (1966). It undermines the *Miranda* warning and obscures its meaning. The plurality opinion is correct to conclude that statements obtained through the use of this technique are inadmissible. Although I agree with much in the careful and convincing opinion for the plurality, my approach does differ in some respects, requiring this separate statement.

The *Miranda* rule has become an important and accepted element of the criminal justice system. See *Dickerson* v. *United States,* 530 U.S. 428, 120 S. Ct. 2326 (2000). At the same time, not every violation of the rule requires suppression of the evidence obtained. Evidence is admissible when the central concerns of *Miranda* are not likely to be implicated and when other objectives of the criminal justice system are best served by its introduction. Thus, we have held that statements obtained in violation of the rule can be used for impeachment, so that the truth finding function of the trial is not distorted by the defense, see *Harris* v. *New York,* 401 U.S. 222, 91 S. Ct. 643 (1971); that there is an exception to protect countervailing concerns of public safety, see *New York* v. *Quarles,* 467 U.S. 649, 104 S. Ct. 2626 (1984); and that physical evidence obtained in reliance on statements taken in violation of the rule is admissible, see *United States* v. *Patane,* __U.S.__, 124 S. Ct 2620 (June 28, 2004). These cases, in my view, are correct. They recognize that admission of evidence is proper when it would further important objectives without compromising *Miranda*'s central concerns. Under these precedents, the scope of the *Miranda* suppression remedy depends on a consideration of those legitimate interests and on whether admission of the evidence under the circumstances would frustrate *Miranda*'s central concerns and objectives. . . .

In my view, *Elstad* was correct in its reasoning and its result. *Elstad* reflects a balanced and pragmatic approach to enforcement of the *Miranda* warning. An officer may not realize that a suspect is in custody and warnings are required. The officer may not plan to question the suspect or may be waiting for a more appropriate time. Skilled investigators often interview suspects multiple times, and good police work may involve referring to prior statements to test their veracity or to refresh recollection. In light of these realities it would be extravagant to treat the presence of one statement that cannot be admitted under *Miranda* as sufficient reason to prohibit subsequent statements preceded by a proper warning. . . .

. . . the interrogating officer here relied on the defendant's prewarning statement to obtain the postwarning statement used against her at trial. The postwarning interview resembled a cross-examination. The officer confronted the defendant with her inadmissible prewarning statements and pushed her to acknowledge them. See App. 70 (" 'Trice, didn't you tell me that he was supposed to die in his sleep?"). This shows the temptations for abuse inherent in the two-step technique. Reference to the prewarning statement was an implicit suggestion that the mere repetition of the earlier statement was not independently incriminating. The implicit suggestion was false.

The technique used in this case distorts the meaning of *Miranda* and furthers no legitimate countervailing interest. The *Miranda* rule would be frustrated were we to allow police to undermine its meaning and effect. The technique simply creates too high a risk that postwarning statements will be obtained when a suspect was deprived of "knowledge essential to his ability to understand the nature of his rights and the consequences of abandoning them." *Moran* v. *Burbine*, 475 U.S. 412, 423–424, 106 S. Ct. 1135 (1986). When an interrogator uses this deliberate, two-step strategy, predicated upon violating *Miranda* during an extended interview, postwarning statements that are related to the substance of prewarning statements must be excluded absent specific, curative steps.

The plurality concludes that whenever a two-stage interview occurs, admissibility of the postwarning statement should depend on "whether the *Miranda* warnings delivered midstream could have been effective enough to accomplish their object" given the specific facts of the case. This test envisions an objective inquiry from the perspective of the suspect, and applies in the case of both intentional and unintentional two-stage interrogations. In my view, this test cuts too broadly. *Miranda's* clarity is one of its strengths, and a multifactor test that applies to every two-stage interrogation may serve to undermine that clarity. Cf. *Berkemer* v. *McCarty*, 468 U.S. 420, 430, 104 S. Ct. 3138 (1984). I would apply a narrower test applicable only in the infrequent case, such as we have here, in which the two-step interrogation technique was used in a calculated way to undermine the *Miranda* warning.

The admissibility of postwarning statements should continue to be governed by the principles of *Elstad* unless the deliberate two-step strategy was employed. If the deliberate two-step strategy has been used, postwarning statements that are related to the substance of prewarning statements must be excluded unless curative measures are taken before the postwarning statement is made. Curative measures should be designed to ensure that a reasonable person in the suspect's situation would understand the import and effect of the *Miranda* warning and of the *Miranda* waiver. For example, a substantial break in time and circumstances between the prewarning statement and the *Miranda* warning may suffice in most circumstances, as it allows the accused to distinguish the two contexts and appreciate that the interrogation has taken a new turn. Cf. *Westover* v. *United States*, decided with *Miranda* v. *Arizona*, 384 U.S. 436, 86 S. Ct. 1602 (1966). Alternatively, an additional warning that explains the likely inadmissibility of the prewarning custodial statement may be sufficient. No curative steps were taken in this case, however, so the postwarning statements are inadmissible and the conviction cannot stand.

For these reasons, I concur in the judgment of the Court.

■ DISSENT: JUSTICE O'CONNOR, with whom THE CHIEF JUSTICE, JUSTICE SCALIA, and JUSTICE THOMAS join, dissenting.

The plurality devours *Oregon v. Elstad,* 470 U.S. 298, 105 S. Ct. 1285 (1985), even as it accuses petitioner's argument of "disfiguring" that decision. I believe that we are bound by *Elstad* to reach a different result, and I would vacate the judgment of the Supreme Court of Missouri.

I

On two preliminary questions I am in full agreement with the plurality. First, the plurality appropriately follows *Elstad* in concluding that Seibert's statement cannot be held inadmissible under a "fruit of the poisonous tree" theory. Second, the plurality correctly declines to focus its analysis on the subjective intent of the interrogating officer.

A

This Court has made clear that there simply is no place for a robust deterrence doctrine with regard to violations of *Miranda v. Arizona,* 384 U.S. 436, 86 S. Ct. 1602 (1966). See *Dickerson* v. *United States,* 530 U.S. 428, 441, 20 S. Ct. 2326 (2000) ("Our decision in *[Elstad]*—refusing to apply the traditional 'fruits' doctrine developed in Fourth Amendment cases— ... simply recognizes the fact that unreasonable searches under the Fourth Amendment are different from unwarned interrogation under the Fifth Amendment"); *Elstad, supra,* at 306, 84 L. Ed. 2d 222, 105 S. Ct. 1285 (unlike the Fourth Amendment exclusionary rule, the "*Miranda* exclusionary rule ... serves the Fifth Amendment and sweeps more broadly than the Fifth Amendment itself"); see also *United States* v. *Patane,* ___ U.S. ___ , 124 S. Ct. 2620 (June 28, 2004) (Kennedy, J., concurring in judgment) (refusal to suppress evidence obtained following an unwarned confession in *Elstad, New York v. Quarles,* 467 U.S. 649, 104 S. Ct. 2626 (1984), and *Harris* v. *New York,* 401 U.S. 222, 91 S. Ct. 643 (1971), was based on "our recognition that the concerns underlying the *Miranda* ... rule and other objectives of the criminal justice system must be accommodated"). Consistent with that view, the Court today refuses to apply the traditional "fruits" analysis to the physical fruit of a claimed *Miranda* violation. *Patane.* The plurality correctly refuses to apply a similar analysis to testimonial fruits.

Although the analysis the plurality ultimately espouses examines the same facts and circumstances that a "fruits" analysis would consider (such as the lapse of time between the two interrogations and change of questioner or location), it does so for entirely different reasons. The fruits analysis would examine those factors because they are relevant to the balance of deterrence value versus the "drastic and socially costly course" of excluding reliable evidence. *Nix* v. *Williams,* 467 U.S. 431, 442–443, 104 S. Ct. 2501 (1984). The plurality, by contrast, looks to those factors to inform the *psychological* judgment regarding whether the suspect has been informed effectively of her right to remain silent. The analytical underpinnings of the two approaches are thus entirely distinct, and they should not be conflated just because they function similarly in practice. Cf. (concurring opinion) (emphasis in original).

B

The plurality's rejection of an intent-based test is also, in my view, correct. Freedom from compulsion lies at the heart of the Fifth Amendment, and requires us to assess whether a suspect's decision to speak truly was voluntary. Because voluntariness is a matter of the suspect's state of mind, we focus our analysis on the way in which suspects experience interrogation. See generally *Miranda*, 384 U.S., at 455, 86 S. Ct. 1602 (summarizing psychological tactics used by police that "undermine" the suspect's "will to resist," and noting that "the very fact of custodial interrogation ... trades on the weakness of individuals");(cite omitted) ("In-custody interrogation of persons suspected or accused of crime contains inherently compelling pressures which work to undermine the individual's will to resist and to compel him to speak where he would not otherwise do so freely").

Thoughts kept inside a police officer's head cannot affect that experience. See *Moran* v. *Burbine,* 475 U.S. 412,106 S. Ct. 1135 (1986) ("Events occurring outside of the presence of the suspect and entirely unknown to him surely can have no bearing on the capacity to comprehend and knowingly relinquish a constitutional right"). In *Moran*, an attorney hired by the suspect's sister had been trying to contact the suspect and was told by the police, falsely, that they would not begin an interrogation that night (cite omitted). The suspect was not aware that an attorney had been hired for him (cite omitted). We rejected an analysis under which a different result would obtain for "the same defendant, armed with the same information and confronted with precisely the same police conduct" if something not known to the defendant—such as the fact that an attorney was attempting to contact him—had been different (cite omitted). The same principle applies here. A suspect who experienced the exact same interrogation as Seibert, save for a difference in the undivulged, subjective intent of the interrogating officer when he failed to give *Miranda* warnings, would not experience the interrogation any differently. "Whether intentional or inadvertent, the state of mind of the police is irrelevant to the question of the intelligence and voluntariness of respondent's election to abandon his rights. Although highly inappropriate, even deliberate deception of an attorney could not possibly affect a suspect's decision to waive his *Miranda* rights unless he were at least aware of the incident" (cite omitted). Cf. *Stansbury* v. *California,* 511 U.S. 318, 324–325, 114 S. Ct. 1526 (1994) *(per curiam)* (police officer's subjective intent is irrelevant to whether suspect is in custody for *Miranda* purposes; "one cannot expect the person under interrogation to probe the officer's innermost thoughts").

Because the isolated fact of Officer Hanrahan's intent could not have had any bearing on Seibert's "capacity to comprehend and knowingly relinquish" her right to remain silent, *Moran*, (cite omitted), it could not by itself affect the voluntariness of her confession. Moreover, recognizing an exception to *Elstad* for intentional violations would require focusing constitutional analysis on a police officer's subjective intent, an unattractive proposition that we all but uniformly avoid. In general, "we believe that 'sending state and federal courts on an expedition into the minds of police officers would produce a grave and fruitless misallocation of judicial resources.' " *United States* v. *Leon,* 468 U.S. 897, 922, n. 23, 104 S. Ct. 3405 (1984) (quoting *Massachusetts* v. *Painten,* 389 U.S. 560, 565, 88 S. Ct. 660 (1968) *(per curiam)* (White, J., dissenting)). This case presents the uncommonly straightforward circumstance of an officer openly admitting that the violation was intentional. But the inquiry will be complicated in other situations probably more likely to occur. For example, different officers involved in an interrogation might claim different states of mind regarding the failure to give *Miranda* warnings. Even in the simple case of a single officer who claims that a failure to give *Miranda* warnings was inadvertent, the likelihood of error will be high. See W. LaFave, Search and Seizure § 1.4(e), p. 124 (3d ed. 1996) ("There is no reason to believe that courts can with any degree of success determine in which instances the police had an ulterior motive").

These evidentiary difficulties have led us to reject an intent-based test in several criminal procedure contexts. For example, in *New York* v. *Quarles,* 467 U.S. 649, 104 S. Ct. 2626 (1984), one of the factors that led us to reject an inquiry into the subjective intent of the police officer in crafting a test for the "public safety" exception to *Miranda* was that officers' motives will be "largely unverifiable" (cite omitted). Similarly, our opinion in *Whren* v. *United States,* 517 U.S. 806, 813–814, 116 S. Ct. 1769 (1996), made clear that "the evidentiary difficulty of establishing subjective intent" was one of the reasons (albeit not the principal one) for refusing to consider intent in Fourth Amendment challenges generally.

For these reasons, I believe that the approach espoused by Justice Kennedy is ill advised. Justice Kennedy would extend *Miranda*'s exclusionary rule to any case in which the use of the "two-step interrogation technique" was "deliberate" or "calculated."(opinion concurring in judgment). This approach untethers the analysis from facts knowable to, and therefore having any potential directly to affect, the suspect. Far from promoting "clarity," *ibid.*, the approach will add a third step to the suppression inquiry. In virtually every two-stage interrogation case, in addition to addressing the standard *Miranda* and voluntariness questions, courts will be forced to conduct the kind of difficult, state-of-mind inquiry that we normally take pains to avoid.

II

The plurality's adherence to *Elstad,* and mine to the plurality, end there. Our decision in *Elstad* rejected two lines of argument advanced in favor of suppression. The first was based on the "fruit of the poisonous tree" doctrine, discussed above. The second was the argument that the "lingering compulsion" inherent in a defendant's having let the "cat out of the bag" required suppression (cite omitted). The Court of Appeals of Oregon, in accepting the latter argument, had endorsed a theory indistinguishable from the one today's plurality adopts: "The coercive impact of the unconstitutionally obtained statement remains, because in a defendant's mind it has sealed his fate. It is this impact that must be dissipated in order to make a subsequent confession admissible" (cite omitted).

We rejected this theory outright. We did so not because we refused to recognize the "psychological impact of the suspect's conviction that he has let the cat out of the bag,'' but because we refused to ''endow'' those ''psychological effects'' with ''constitutional implications.'' (cite omitted).To do so, we said, would ''effectively immunize a suspect who responds to pre-*Miranda* warning questions from the consequences of his subsequent informed waiver,'' an immunity that ''comes at a high cost to legitimate law enforcement activity, while adding little desirable protection to the individual's interest in not being *compelled* to testify against himself'' (cite omitted). . . .

I would analyze the two-step interrogation procedure under the voluntariness standards central to the Fifth Amendment and reiterated in *Elstad*. *Elstad* commands that if Seibert's first statement is shown to have been involuntary, the court must examine whether the taint dissipated through the passing of time or a change in circumstances: ''When a prior statement is actually coerced, the time that passes between confessions, the change in place of interrogations, and the change in identity of the interrogators all bear on whether that coercion has carried over into the second confession.'' (cite omitted). In addition, Seibert's second statement should be suppressed if she showed that it was involuntary despite the *Miranda* warnings. *Elstad* (cite omitted). (''The relevant inquiry is whether, in fact, the second statement was also voluntarily made. As in any such inquiry, the finder of fact must examine the surrounding circumstances and the entire course of police conduct with respect to the suspect in evaluating the voluntariness of his statements''). Although I would leave this analysis for the Missouri courts to conduct on remand, I note that, unlike the officers in *Elstad*, Officer Hanrahan referred to Seibert's unwarned statement during the second part of the interrogation when she made a statement at odds with her unwarned confession. App. 70 ('' 'Trice, didn't you tell me that he was supposed to die in his sleep?''); cf. *Elstad* (cite omitted) (officers did not ''exploit the unwarned admission to pressure respondent into waiving his right to remain silent''). Such a tactic may bear on the voluntariness inquiry . . . (cites omitted).

Because I believe that the plurality gives insufficient deference to *Elstad* and that Justice Kennedy places improper weight on subjective intent, I respectfully dissent.

* * *

CHAPTER 9

RIGHTS OF INDIGENTS

B. TRIAL COUNSEL: THE SIXTH AMENDMENT APPROACH

Add at end of note 1 on page 792:

In *Alabama v. Shelton*, 535 U.S. 654, 122 S.Ct. 1764 (2002), the defendant was convicted of third-degree assault. The court imposed a 30 day jail sentence, but then immediately suspended it and placed Shelton on probation for two years. Was he entitled to the Sixth Amendment right to appointed counsel under the *Argersinger* and *Scott* opinions?

The Court, in a 5–4 opinion, held that he was entitled to state-appointed counsel.

Justice Ginsberg, writing for the majority, rejected the notions that this would impede a state's ability to impose probation and that it would cause states to incur additional expenses. Instead, the potential for imprisonment upon a probation violation required counsel to be provided.

Justice Scalia, writing for the dissent (joined by Chief Justice Rehnquist, and Justices Kennedy and Thomas) disagreed, urging that counsel be required only upon actual imprisonment.

CHAPTER 10

The Preliminary Hearing

Add to end of notes on page 826 after Counter of Riverside v. McLaughlin:

4. Congress may not eliminate the need for a prompt preliminary hearing or grand jury presentment by classifying those held as enemy combatants. The detained individual must be given an opportunity rebut the Government's factual allegations before a neutral fact-finder. *Hamdi v. Rumsfeld,* ___ U.S. ___, 124 S.Ct. 2633 (2004).

CHAPTER 13

PRE-TRIAL MOTIONS

A. DISMISSAL FOR DOUBLE JEOPARDY & RELATED PRINCIPLES

Add as note 3 at the top of page 925:

3. In *Smith v. Doe*, 538 U.S. 84, 123 S.Ct. 1140 (2003), the Court upheld the constitutionality of the Alaska Sex Offender Registration Law against claims that it violated double jeopardy.

CHAPTER 19

Presenting the Case—Problems Encountered

E. Cross-Examination and Impeachment

1. The Ordinary Witness

Page 1444, before Delaware v. Fensterer, add (New Main Case)

Crawford v. Washington

Supreme Court of the United States, 2004.
___ U.S. ___, 124 S.Ct. 1354.

■ Justice Scalia delivered the opinion of the Court.

Petitioner Michael Crawford stabbed a man who allegedly tried to rape his wife, Sylvia. At his trial, the State played for the jury Sylvia's tape-recorded statement to the police describing the stabbing, even though he had no opportunity for cross-examination. The Washington Supreme Court upheld petitioner's conviction after determining that Sylvia's statement was reliable....

* * *

The State charged petitioner with assault and attempted murder. At trial, he claimed self-defense. Sylvia did not testify because of the state marital privilege, which generally bars a spouse from testifying without the other spouse's consent. In Washington, this privilege does not extend to a spouse's out-of-court statements admissible under a hearsay exception, so the State sought to introduce Sylvia's tape-recorded statements to the police as evidence that the stabbing was not in self-defense. Noting that Sylvia had admitted she led petitioner to Lee's apartment and thus had facilitated the assault, the State invoked the hearsay exception for statements against penal interest, Wash. Rule Evid. 804(b)(3) (2003).

* * *

II

Ohio v. Roberts says that an unavailable witness's out-of-court statement may be admitted so long as it has adequate indicia of reliability—*i.e.*, falls within a "firmly rooted hearsay exception" or bears "particularized guarantees of trustworthiness." Petitioner argues that this test strays from the original meaning of the Confrontation Clause and urges us to reconsider it.

The Constitution's text does not alone resolve this case. One could plausibly read "witnesses against" a defendant to mean those who actually testify at trial, cf. *Woodsides v. State,* 3 Miss. 655, 664–665 (1837), those whose statements are offered at trial, see 3 J. Wigmore, Evidence § 1397, p. 104 (2d ed.1923) (hereinafter Wigmore), or something in-between. We must therefore turn to the historical background of the Clause to understand its meaning.

* * *

III

History supports two inferences about the meaning of the Sixth Amendment.

First, the principal evil at which the Confrontation Clause was directed was the civil-law mode of criminal procedure, and particularly its use of *ex parte* examinations as evidence against the accused. It was these practices that the Crown deployed in notorious treason cases like Raleigh's; that the Marian statutes invited; that English law's assertion of a right to confrontation was meant to prohibit; and that the founding-era rhetoric decried....

Accordingly, we once again reject the view that the Confrontation Clause applies of its own force only to in-court testimony, and that its application to out-of-court statements introduced at trial depends upon "the law of Evidence for the time being." 3 Wigmore § 1397, at 101; accord, *Dutton v. Evans,* 400 U.S. 74, 94, 91 S.Ct. 210, 27 L.Ed.2d 213 (1970) (Harlan, J., concurring in result). Leaving the regulation of out-of-court statements to the law of evidence would render the Confrontation Clause powerless to prevent even the most flagrant inquisitorial practices....

* * *

The text of the Confrontation Clause reflects this focus. It applies to "witnesses" against the accused—in other words, those who "bear testimony." 1 N. Webster, An American Dictionary of the English Language (1828). "Testimony," in turn, is typically "[a] solemn declaration or affirmation made for the purpose of establishing or proving some fact." *Ibid.* An accuser who makes a formal statement to government officers bears testimony in a sense that a person who makes a casual remark to an acquaintance does not. The constitutional text, like the history underlying the common-law right of confrontation, thus reflects an especially acute concern with a specific type of out-of-court statement.

* * *

Statements taken by police officers in the course of interrogations are also testimonial under even a narrow standard....

* * *

The historical record also supports a second proposition: that the Framers would not have allowed admission of testimonial statements of a witness who did not appear at trial unless he was unavailable to testify, and the defendant had had a prior opportunity for cross-examination. The text of the Sixth Amendment does not suggest any open-ended exceptions from the confrontation requirement to be developed by the courts. Rather, the "right . . . to be confronted with the witnesses against him," Amdt. 6, is most naturally read as a reference to the right of confrontation at common law, admitting only those exceptions established at the time of the founding. See *Mattox v. United States,* 156 U.S. 237, 243, 15 S.Ct. 337, 39 L.Ed. 409 (1895). . . .

We do not read the historical sources to say that a prior opportunity to cross-examine was merely a sufficient, rather than a necessary, condition for admissibility of testimonial statements. They suggest that this requirement was dispositive, and not merely one of several ways to establish reliability. This is not to deny, as THE CHIEF JUSTICE notes, that "[t]here were always exceptions to the general rule of exclusion" of hearsay evidence. Several had become well established by 1791. See 3 Wigmore § 1397, at 101. But there is scant evidence that exceptions were invoked to admit *testimonial* statements against the accused in a *criminal* case. Most of the hearsay exceptions covered statements that by their nature were not testimonial—for example, business records or statements in furtherance of a conspiracy. We do not infer from these that the Framers thought exceptions would apply even to prior testimony. Cf. *Lilly v. Virginia,* 527 U.S. 116, 134, 119 S.Ct. 1887, 144 L.Ed.2d 117 (1999) (plurality opinion) ("[A]ccomplices' confessions that inculpate a criminal defendant are not within a firmly rooted exception to the hearsay rule").

* * *

Even our recent cases, in their outcomes, hew closely to the traditional line. *Ohio v. Roberts,* 448 U.S., at 67–70, 100 S.Ct. 2531, admitted testimony from a preliminary hearing at which the defendant had examined the witness. *Lilly v. Virginia, supra,* excluded testimonial statements that the defendant had had no opportunity to test by cross-examination. . . .

V

Although the results of our decisions have generally been faithful to the original meaning of the Confrontation Clause, the same cannot be said of our rationales. *Roberts* conditions the admissibility of all hearsay evidence on whether it falls under a "firmly rooted hearsay exception" or bears "particularized guarantees of trustworthiness." 448 U.S., at 66, 100 S.Ct. 2531. This test departs from the historical principles identified above in two respects. First, it is too broad: It applies the same mode of analysis whether or not the hearsay consists of *ex parte* testimony. This often results in close constitutional scrutiny in cases that are far removed from the core concerns of the Clause. At the same time, however, the test is too narrow: It admits statements that *do* consist of *ex parte* testimony upon a mere finding of reliability. This malleable standard often fails to protect against paradigmatic confrontation violations.

* * *

Where testimonial statements are involved, we do not think the Framers meant to leave the Sixth Amendment's protection to the vagaries of the rules of evidence, much less to amorphous notions of "reliability." Certainly none of the authorities discussed above acknowledges any general reliability exception to the common-law rule. Admitting statements deemed reliable by a judge is fundamentally at odds with the right of confrontation. To be sure, the Clause's ultimate goal is to ensure reliability of evidence, but it is a procedural rather than a substantive guarantee. It commands, not that evidence be reliable, but that reliability be assessed in a particular manner: by testing in the crucible of cross-examination. The Clause thus reflects a judgment, not only about the desirability of reliable evidence (a point on which there could be little dissent), but about how reliability can best be determined....

The *Roberts* test allows a jury to hear evidence, untested by the adversary process, based on a mere judicial determination of reliability. It thus replaces the constitutionally prescribed method of assessing reliability with a wholly foreign one. In this respect, it is very different from exceptions to the Confrontation Clause that make no claim to be a surrogate means of assessing reliability....

* * *

Dispensing with confrontation because testimony is obviously reliable is akin to dispensing with jury trial because a defendant is obviously guilty. This is not what the Sixth Amendment prescribes.

B

The legacy of *Roberts* in other courts vindicates the Framers' wisdom in rejecting a general reliability exception. The framework is so unpredictable that it fails to provide meaningful protection from even core confrontation violations.

Reliability is an amorphous, if not entirely subjective, concept. There are countless factors bearing on whether a statement is reliable; the nine-factor balancing test applied by the Court of Appeals below is representative. See, *e.g., People v. Farrell,* 34 P.3d 401, 406–407 (Colo.2001) (eight-factor test). Whether a statement is deemed reliable depends heavily on which factors the judge considers and how much weight he accords each of them. Some courts wind up attaching the same significance to opposite facts. For example, the Colorado Supreme Court held a statement more reliable because its inculpation of the defendant was "detailed," *id.,* at 407, while the Fourth Circuit found a statement more reliable because the portion implicating another was "fleeting," *United States v. Photogrammetric Data Servs., Inc.,* 259 F.3d 229, 245 (C.A.4 2001). The Virginia Court of Appeals found a statement more reliable because the witness was in custody and charged with a crime (thus making the statement more obviously against her penal interest), see *Nowlin v. Commonwealth,* 40 Va.App. 327, 335–338, 579 S.E.2d 367, 371–372 (2003), while the Wisconsin Court of Appeals found a statement more reliable because the witness was *not* in custody and *not* a suspect, see *State v. Bintz,* 2002 WI App. 204, ¶ 13, 257 Wis.2d 177, 187, 650 N.W.2d 913, 918. Finally, the Colorado Supreme Court in one case found a statement more reliable because it was given "immediately after" the events at issue, *Farrell, supra,* at 407, while that same court, in another case, found a statement more reliable because two years had elapsed, *Stevens v. People,* 29 P.3d 305, 316 (Colo.2001).

The unpardonable vice of the *Roberts* test, however, is not its unpredictability, but its demonstrated capacity to admit core testimonial statements that the Confrontation Clause plainly meant to exclude. Despite the plurality's speculation in *Lilly,* 527 U.S., at 137, 119 S.Ct. 1887, that it was "highly unlikely" that accomplice confessions implicating the accused could survive *Roberts,* courts continue routinely to admit them.... One recent study found that, after *Lilly,* appellate courts admitted accomplice statements to the authorities in 25 out of 70 cases—more than one-third of the time. Kirst, Appellate Court Answers to the Confrontation Questions in *Lilly v. Virginia,* 53 Syracuse L.Rev. 87, 105 (2003). Courts have invoked *Roberts* to admit other sorts of plainly testimonial statements despite the absence of any opportunity to cross-examine.

To add insult to injury, some of the courts that admit untested testimonial statements find reliability in the very factors that *make* the statements testimonial.... One court relied on the fact that the witness's statement was made to police while in custody on pending charges—the theory being that this made the statement more clearly against penal interest and thus more reliable. Other courts routinely rely on the fact that a prior statement is given under oath in judicial proceedings. That inculpating statements are given in a testimonial setting is not an antidote to the confrontation problem, but rather the trigger that makes the Clause's demands most urgent. It is not enough to point out that most of the usual safeguards of the adversary process attend the statement, when the single safeguard missing is the one the Confrontation Clause demands.

Roberts' failings were on full display in the proceedings below. Sylvia Crawford made her statement while in police custody, herself a potential suspect in the case. Indeed, she had been told that whether she would be released "depend[ed] on how the investigation continues." App. 81. In response to often leading questions from police detectives, she implicated her husband in Lee's stabbing and at least arguably undermined his self-defense claim. Despite all this, the trial court admitted her statement, listing several reasons why it was reliable. In its opinion reversing, the Court of Appeals listed several *other* reasons why the statement was *not* reliable. Finally, the State Supreme Court relied exclusively on the interlocking character of the statement and disregarded every other factor the lower courts had considered. The case is thus a self-contained demonstration of *Roberts'* unpredictable and inconsistent application.

Each of the courts also made assumptions that cross-examination might well have undermined. The trial court, for example, stated that Sylvia Crawford's statement was reliable because she was an eyewitness with direct knowledge of the events. But Sylvia at one point told the police that she had "shut [her] eyes and ... didn't really watch" part of the fight, and that she was "in shock." The trial court also buttressed its reliability finding by claiming that Sylvia was "being questioned by law enforcement, and, thus, the [questioner] is ... neutral to her and not someone who would be inclined to advance her interests and shade her version of the truth unfavorably toward the defendant." The Framers would be astounded to learn that *ex parte* testimony could be admitted against a criminal defendant because it was elicited by "neutral" government officers. But even if the court's assessment of the officer's motives was accurate, it says nothing about Sylvia's perception of her situation. Only cross-examination could reveal that.

* * *

We readily concede that we could resolve this case by simply reweighing the "reliability factors" under *Roberts* and finding that Sylvia Crawford's statement falls short. But we view this as one of those rare cases in which the result below is so improbable that it reveals a fundamental failure on our part to interpret the Constitution in a way that secures its intended constraint on judicial discretion. Moreover, to reverse the Washington Supreme Court's decision after conducting our own reliability analysis would perpetuate, not avoid, what the Sixth Amendment condemns. The Constitution prescribes a procedure for determining the reliability of testimony in criminal trials, and we, no less than the state courts, lack authority to replace it with one of our own devising.

We have no doubt that the courts below were acting in utmost good faith when they found reliability. The Framers, however, would not have been content to indulge this assumption. They knew that judges, like other government officers, could not always be trusted to safeguard the rights of the people; the likes of the dread Lord Jeffreys were not yet too distant a memory. They were loath to leave too much discretion in judicial hands. Cf. U.S. Const., Amdt. 6 (criminal jury trial); Amdt. 7 (civil jury trial); By replacing categorical constitutional guarantees with open-ended balancing tests, we do violence to their design. Vague standards are manipulable, and, while that might be a small concern in run-of-the-mill assault prosecutions like this one, the Framers had an eye toward politically charged cases like Raleigh's—great state trials where the impartiality of even those at the highest levels of the judiciary might not be so clear. It is difficult to imagine *Roberts'* providing any meaningful protection in those circumstances.

* * *

Where nontestimonial hearsay is at issue, it is wholly consistent with the Framers' design to afford the States flexibility in their development of hearsay law—as does *Roberts,* and as would an approach that exempted such statements from Confrontation Clause scrutiny altogether. Where testimonial evidence is at issue, however, the Sixth Amendment demands what the common law required: unavailability and a prior opportunity for cross-examination. We leave for another day any effort to spell out a comprehensive definition of "testimonial." Whatever else the term covers, it applies at a minimum to prior testimony at a preliminary hearing, before a grand jury, or at a former trial; and to police interrogations. These are the modern practices with closest kinship to the abuses at which the Confrontation Clause was directed.

In this case, the State admitted Sylvia's testimonial statement against petitioner, despite the fact that he had no opportunity to cross-examine her. That alone is sufficient to make out a violation of the Sixth Amendment. *Roberts* notwithstanding, we decline to mine the record in search of indicia of reliability. Where testimonial statements are at issue, the only indicium of reliability sufficient to satisfy constitutional demands is the one the Constitution actually prescribes: confrontation.

The judgment of the Washington Supreme Court is reversed, and the case is remanded for further proceedings not inconsistent with this opinion.

It is so ordered.

■ CHIEF JUSTICE REHNQUIST, with whom JUSTICE O'CONNOR joins, concurring in the judgment.

I dissent from the Court's decision to overrule *Ohio v. Roberts,* 448 U.S. 56, 100 S.Ct. 2531, 65 L.Ed.2d 597 (1980). I believe that the Court's adoption of a new interpretation of the Confrontation Clause is not backed by sufficiently persuasive reasoning to overrule long-established precedent. Its decision casts a mantle of uncertainty over future criminal trials in both federal and state courts, and is by no means necessary to decide the present case.

The Court's distinction between testimonial and nontestimonial statements, contrary to its claim, is no better rooted in history than our current doctrine. Under the common law, although the courts were far from consistent, out-of-court statements made by someone other than the accused and not taken under oath, unlike *ex parte* depositions or affidavits, were generally not considered substantive evidence upon which a conviction could be based. See, *e.g., King v. Brasier,* 1 Leach 199, 200, 168 Eng. Rep. 202 (K.B.1779); see also J. Langbein, Origins of Adversary Criminal Trial 235–242 (2003); G. Gilbert, Evidence 152 (3d ed. 1769). Testimonial statements such as accusatory statements to police officers likely would have been disapproved of in the 18th century, not necessarily because they resembled *ex parte* affidavits or depositions as the Court reasons, but more likely than not because they were not made under oath. See *King v. Woodcock,* 1 Leach 500, 503, 168 Eng. Rep. 352, 353 (1789) (noting that a statement taken by a justice of the peace may not be admitted into evidence unless taken under oath). Without an oath, one usually did not get to the second step of whether confrontation was required.

* * *

Thus, while I agree that the Framers were mainly concerned about sworn affidavits and depositions, it does not follow that they were similarly concerned about the Court's broader category of testimonial statements. See 1 N. Webster, An American Dictionary of the English Language (1828) (defining "Testimony" as "[a] solemn declaration or affirmation made for the purpose of establishing or proving some fact. *Such affirmation in judicial proceedings, may be verbal or written, but must be under oath* "(emphasis added)). As far as I can tell, unsworn testimonial statements were treated no differently at common law than were nontestimonial statements, and it seems to me any classification of statements as testimonial beyond that of sworn affidavits and depositions will be somewhat arbitrary, merely a proxy for what the Framers might have intended had such evidence been liberally admitted as substantive evidence like it is today.

I therefore see no reason why the distinction the Court draws is preferable to our precedent. Starting with Chief Justice Marshall's interpretation as a Circuit Justice in 1807, 16 years after the ratification of the Sixth Amendment, *United States v. Burr,* 25 F.Cas. 187, 193 (No. 14,694) (CC Va. 1807), continuing with our cases in the late 19th century, *Mattox v. United States,* 156 U.S. 237, 243–244, 15 S.Ct. 337, 39 L.Ed. 409 (1895); *Kirby v. United States,* 174 U.S. 47, 54–57, 19 S.Ct. 574, 43 L.Ed. 890 (1899), and through today, *e.g., White v. Illinois,* 502 U.S. 346, 352–353, 112 S.Ct. 736, 116 L.Ed.2d 848 (1992), we have never drawn a distinction between testimonial and nontestimonial statements. And for that matter, neither has any other court of which I am aware. I see little value in trading our precedent for an imprecise approximation at this late date.

I am also not convinced that the Confrontation Clause categorically requires the exclusion of testimonial statements. Although many States had their own Confrontation Clauses, they were of recent vintage and were not interpreted with any regularity before 1791. State cases that recently followed the ratification of the Sixth Amendment were not uniform; the Court itself cites state cases from the early 19th century that took a more stringent view of the right to confrontation than does the Court, prohibiting former testimony even if the witness was subjected to cross-examination. See *ante,* at 1363 (citing *Finn v. Commonwealth,* 26 Va. 701, 708 (1827); *State v. Atkins,* 1 Tenn. 229 (1807) *(per curiam)*).

* * *

Between 1700 and 1800 the rules regarding the admissibility of out-of-court statements were still being developed. There were always exceptions to the general rule of exclusion, and it is not clear to me that the Framers categorically wanted to eliminate further ones. It is one thing to trace the right of confrontation back to the Roman Empire; it is quite another to conclude that such a right absolutely excludes a large category of evidence. It is an odd conclusion indeed to think that the Framers created a cut-and-dried rule with respect to the admissibility of testimonial statements when the law during their own time was not fully settled.

* * *

Exceptions to confrontation have always been derived from the experience that some out-of-court statements are just as reliable as cross-examined in-court testimony due to the circumstances under which they were made. We have recognized, for example, that co-conspirator statements simply "cannot be replicated, even if the declarant testifies to the same matters in court." *United States v. Inadi,* 475 U.S. 387, 395, 106 S.Ct. 1121, 89 L.Ed.2d 390 (1986). Because the statements are made while the declarant and the accused are partners in an illegal enterprise, the statements are unlikely to be false and their admission "actually furthers the 'Confrontation Clause's very mission' which is to 'advance the accuracy of the truth-determining process in criminal trials.'" *Id.,* at 396, 106 S.Ct. 1121 (quoting *Tennessee v. Street,* 471 U.S. 409, 415, 105 S.Ct. 2078, 85 L.Ed.2d 425 (1985) (some internal quotation marks omitted)). Similar reasons justify the introduction of spontaneous declarations, see *White,* 502 U.S., at 356, 112 S.Ct. 736, statements made in the course of procuring medical services, see *ibid.*, dying declarations, see *Kirby, supra,* at 61, 19 S.Ct. 574, and countless other hearsay exceptions. That a statement might be testimonial does nothing to undermine the wisdom of one of these exceptions.

* * *

In choosing the path it does, the Court of course overrules *Ohio v. Roberts,* 448 U.S. 56, 100 S.Ct. 2531, 65 L.Ed.2d 597 (1980), a case decided nearly a quarter of a century ago. *Stare decisis* is not an inexorable command in the area of constitutional law, see *Payne v. Tennessee,* 501 U.S. 808, 828, 111 S.Ct. 2597, 115 L.Ed.2d 720 (1991), but by and large, it "is the preferred course because it promotes the evenhanded, predictable, and consistent development of legal principles, fosters reliance on judicial decisions, and contributes to the actual and perceived integrity of the judicial process," *id.,* at 827, 111 S.Ct. 2597. And in making this appraisal, doubt that the new rule is indeed the "right" one should surely be weighed in the balance. Though there are no vested interests involved, unresolved questions for the future of everyday criminal trials throughout the country surely counsel the same sort of caution. The Court grandly declares that "[w]e leave for another day any effort to spell out a comprehensive definition of 'testimonial,' "*ante,* at 1374. But the thousands of federal prosecutors and the tens of thousands of state prosecutors need answers as to what beyond the specific kinds of "testimony" the Court lists, see *ibid.,* is covered by the new rule. They need them now, not months or years from now. Rules of criminal evidence are applied every day in courts throughout the country, and parties should not be left in the dark in this manner.

To its credit, the Court's analysis of "testimony" excludes at least some hearsay exceptions, such as business records and official records. To hold otherwise would require numerous additional witnesses without any apparent gain in the truth-seeking process. Likewise to the Court's credit is its implicit recognition that the mistaken application of its new rule by courts which guess wrong as to the scope of the rule is subject to harmless-error analysis.

But these are palliatives to what I believe is a mistaken change of course. It is a change of course not in the least necessary to reverse the judgment of the Supreme Court of Washington in this case. The result the Court reaches follows inexorably from *Roberts* and its progeny without any need for overruling that line of cases....

Page 1505, add after "A Note on Consistency" (New Main Case)

Stumpf v. Mitchell

United States Court of Appeals, Sixth Circuit, 2004.
367 F.3d 594.

■ DAUGHTREY, CIRCUIT JUDGE.

The petitioner, John David Stumpf, is a state prisoner incarcerated on Ohio's death row. He appeals the district court's dismissal of his habeas corpus petition....

Prior to entering a guilty plea, Stumpf had waived his right to a trial by jury and elected to have his case heard by a three-judge panel. Under Ohio law, when a defendant pleads guilty to aggravated murder, the court must hold an evidentiary hearing to establish a factual basis for the plea. The three-judge panel held such a hearing in this case and found that there was a factual basis for Stumpf's plea, that he was guilty of aggravated murder with the capital specification and, ultimately, that there was insufficient mitigating evidence to spare Stumpf from imposition of the death penalty.

* * *

Most of the underlying facts are undisputed in this case and do not affect the legal determinations necessary to the resolution of the appeal.... We adopt the district court's characterization of the facts, as determined by the state courts, as follows:

> On May 14, 1984, Stumpf, Clyde Daniel Wesley, and Norman Leroy Edmonds, after visiting a bar in Washington, Pennsylvania, got on Interstate 70 and headed west toward Ohio. By sundown, they had reached Guernsey County. They stopped their car along I–70 and, leaving Edmonds in the car, Stumpf and Wesley walked to a nearby house under the pretense of needing to make a phone call. The house they chose was owned and occupied by Norman and Mary Jane Stout. Stout admitted Stumpf and Wesley into his home and allowed them to use the phone. When they had completed the call, both Stumpf and Wesley produced pistols and announced a robbery. Stumpf held the Stouts at gunpoint in a back bedroom while Wesley searched the house for items to steal.

At some point, Stout moved toward Stumpf, and Stumpf shot him between the eyes with his pistol. The shot was not fatal, and Stout subsequently pushed Stumpf into the next room. During this altercation, Stout was struck on the head with a pistol and shot in the head a second time. These actions were enough to render him semi-conscious but not to kill him. While lying on the floor in the other room, Stout heard four gunshots. There is no dispute that Mary Jane Stout was shot and killed during the course of this robbery, although there is a dispute as to whether Stumpf or Wesley fired the fatal shots. After Mrs. Stout was killed, Stumpf and Wesley stole the Stout's car and fled. Stumpf was arrested several days later, and after initially denying any knowledge about these crimes and then being told that Stout had survived, he confessed to being involved.

At the time the trial court proceedings occurred, Wesley had not yet been extradited from Texas. However, subsequent to Stumpf's having pleaded guilty and having been sentenced to death, Wesley was convicted of aggravated murder by a jury and received a sentence of life imprisonment without the possibility of parole for 20 years. The State introduced evidence at Wesley's trial that Wesley and not Stumpf fired the shots that killed Mrs. Stout. Edmonds was not charged in the Stout murder and robbery, but was charged for other offenses committed during this crime spree, and he agreed to and did testify against both Stumpf and Wesley concerning the murder of Mary Jane Stout.

* * *

Stumpf argues that the prosecutor's use of two conflicting theories concerning the identity of the shooter to convict both him and Wesley constitutes a due process violation.

The Constitution's Due Process clause guarantees every defendant the right to a fair trial. The Supreme Court has also emphasized that "because the prosecutor is in a peculiar and very definite sense the servant of the law, the twofold aim of which is that guilt shall not escape or innocence suffer ..., it is as much his duty to refrain from improper methods calculated to produce a wrongful conviction as it is to use every legitimate method to bring about one." Berger v. United States, 295 U.S. 78, 88, 55 S.Ct. 629, 79 L.Ed. 1314 (1935), overruled on other grounds, Stirone v. United States, 361 U.S. 212, 80 S.Ct. 270, 4 L.Ed.2d 252 (1960).

Drawing on the principle that the Constitution's "overriding concern [is] with the justice of the finding of guilt," United States v. Agurs, 427 U.S. 97, 112, 96 S.Ct. 2392, 49 L.Ed.2d 342 (1976), several of our sister circuits have found, or implied, that the use of inconsistent, irreconcilable theories to secure convictions against more than one defendant in prosecutions for the same crime violates the due process clause. See, e.g., Smith v. Groose, 205 F.3d 1045 (8th Cir.2000); Thompson v. Calderon, 120 F.3d 1045 (9th Cir.1997) (en banc) vacated on other grounds, 523 U.S. 538, 118 S.Ct. 1489, 140 L.Ed.2d 728 (1998); Drake v. Kemp, 762 F.2d 1449 (11th Cir.1985) (en banc) (Clark, J., specially concurring); cf. Nichols v. Scott, 69 F.3d 1255 (5th Cir.1995) (involving a situation where both defendants had shot at the victim and it was unclear whose bullet had actually hit and killed the victim; the court found that the two theories advanced by the prosecution were not inconsistent because both defendants could have been convicted under the law of parties). On this issue of first impression in this court, we now join our sister circuits in finding that the use of inconsistent, irreconcilable theories to convict two defendants for the same crime is a due process violation.

* * *

In this case, the state clearly used inconsistent, irreconcilable theories at Stumpf's hearings and Wesley's trial At each proceeding, the prosecutor argued that the defendant had been the one to pull the trigger, resulting in the fatal shots to Mary Jane Stout. At Wesley's trial, the prosecutor relied on Eastman's testimony and on the gun-switching scenario argued by Stumpf, to secure Wesley's conviction. The prosecutor asserted:

> Believing he had killed Mr. Stout, [Stumpf] pitched the gun aside and left the immediate area back the hallway down the steps to the basement. At that point [Wesley,] whose own gun was jammed, picked that chrome colored Raven up and as Mrs. Stout sat helplessly on her bed, shot her four times in order to leave no witnesses to the crime.

These statements are irreconcilably inconsistent with those made by the very same prosecutor at Stumpf's plea hearing, when he told the trial court:

> Believing that the had killed Mr. Stout, Stumpf [then] turned the same chrome colored Raven automatic pistol upon Mary Jane Stout as she sat on the bed and shot her four times. Three times in the left side of the head and neck and one time in the writs; obviously in order not to leave anyone available to identify him.

The state claims that, because Eastman's testimony was not available at the time of Stumpf's guilty plea, Stumpf is really asserting Wesley's due process claim in the guise of his own. The state also argues that "it was of no import to the charge of capital murder against Stumpf which of the two [defendants] killed the witness [Mrs. Stout]" since the capital specification was that Mrs. Stout was killed because she was a witness to the crime, and not that the defendant had been the shooter. Finally, the state asserts that inconsistent, irreconcilable theories were not used in these two cases, because the prosecution did not rely on Eastman's testimony at Wesley's trial. None of these arguments is persuasive.

First, Stumpf clearly has a due process claim even though Eastman's testimony was not available at the time of his trial. It is true that this is not a case where the prosecutor selectively presented evidence in Stumpf's case to support the theory of the murder he was arguing in that case. However, the due process challenge to the use of inconsistent theories is based on the notion of fundamental fairness. Because inconsistent theories render convictions unreliable, they constitute a violation of the due process rights of any defendant in whose trial they are used. Furthermore, it is disingenuous of the state to argue that there is no violation of Stumpf's rights because the prosecutor had no knowledge of Eastman's testimony at the time of Stumpf's plea. The state learned of Eastman's testimony soon after Stumpf's plea and sentencing and yet continued to maintain that the convictions of both Stumpf and Wesley, each of which was obtained by arguing that a different individual was the shooter, were sound and reliable. Indeed, the state maintained that Eastman's testimony was unreliable during a hearing on Stumpf's motion to vacate his plea and/or his sentence. To this day, there has been no suggestion of corrective action by the state.

The state's second argument, with which the district court agreed, is that the identity of the shooter was not the critical issue in either trial and that therefore the use of different theories did not violate Stumpf's due process rights. By pleading guilty to capital murder, the state's argument goes, Stumpf admitted concerted action with Wesley in causing the death of Mary Jane Stout for the purposes of avoiding detection. All that was left for the prosecution then to prove, under this theory, was that Mrs. Stout was killed so that the defendant could escape detection for other crimes. But this argument ignores the fact that, as the aggravated murder statute existed in 1984, specific intent was a necessary element of the crime. *See* Ohio Rev.Code § 2903.01(B); Because Stumpf never confessed to specific intent to kill Mrs. Stout, the prosecution bore the burden of proving beyond a reasonable doubt that Stumpf was guilty of the charge.

Finally, the state argues that irreconcilable theories were not used because Eastman's testimony was completely unreliable. State's counsel even asserted at oral argument that the state did not rely on Eastman's testimony in order to prosecute Wesley. This argument is just short of astounding, given the fact that in seeking to convict Wesley of aggravated murder, the prosecution offered no proof of the element of specific intent other than the theory that Wesley was the actual shooter. That the state relied on Eastman's testimony is evident from the fact that it presented his testimony to the jury, and from the fact that it prevented Wesley's counsel from presenting evidence of Stumpf's guilty plea. Had the state presented a theory of the crime consistent with the theory it asserted at Stumpf's evidentiary hearing, it would have had no need to keep that information from Wesley's jury.

The district court ultimately accepted the state's argument that the core issue at Stumpf's evidentiary hearing was not the identity of the shooter. However, in reaching this conclusion, the court started with what we believe to be a faulty assumption, *i.e.,* that "the state was not required to prove that petitioner was the actual shooter." The district court, in concluding that the specification to which Stumpf pleaded guilty, Ohio Rev.Code § 2929.04(A)(3), did not require that Stumpf be proven to be the "principal offender," overlooked, once again, the fact that the aggravated murder statute itself requires specific intent. The state was not required to prove that the petitioner was the actual shooter, but it was required to prove specific intent.

Even proceeding from the district court's false assumption, however, we cannot agree with the court's ultimate conclusion. The district court found that, although the state was not required to prove that Stumpf was the actual shooter, "the fact remains that the state did argue that petitioner was [the] actual shooter and the trial court did find that petitioner was the actual shooter." The district court went on to recognize that the trial court cited this very finding as "a reason, and a very substantial reason" that petitioner received the death penalty. The district court found, however, that habeas relief was not warranted, because the Supreme Court of Ohio's independent reweighing of the aggravating and mitigating circumstances cured any misplaced reliance on Stumpf having been the actual shooter. Apparently engaging in such a reweighing process, the Ohio Supreme Court concluded that Eastman's testimony was not sufficient to tip the balance of aggravating and mitigating factors.

We cannot agree with this reasoning, because we do not believe that a reweighing of the factors used to support imposition of the death penalty cures the due process violation at issue. The Ohio Supreme Court, it is true, found that "the testimony of a cellmate during Clyde Wesley's trial is of minimal credibility, especially in light of appellant's guilty plea and the substantial evidence to the contrary adduced during appellant's sentencing hearing." State v. Stumpf, 32 Ohio St.3d at 106, 512 N.E.2d 598. But, putting aside for the moment the question of whether Eastman's testimony need be credible for a due process violation to be established by the state prosecution's presentation of and evident reliance on it, there is no explicit state court determination regarding Eastman's credibility to which this court must give deference. Although there is a presumption that a state court's factual findings are correct, this presumption applies only to basic facts and to those facts implicitly established through the trial court's unique ability to judge the witnesses' credibility and demeanor. No court at any level considering Stumpf's claims actually observed Eastman's testimony. The first court explicitly to examine the transcripts of that testimony, the two-judge trial panel, failed to make any factual findings, instead denying Stumpf's motion summarily. The Supreme Court of Ohio recognized as much when it found that the trial court had "apparently" determined that Eastman's testimony did not change the balancing of mitigating and aggravating factors. The Supreme Court of Ohio also presumably examined the transcripts, concluding that the testimony was of "minimal credibility." Neither the presumed factual finding by the trial court, nor the more explicit one made by the Supreme Court of Ohio is due the type of complete deference contemplated by the state, because neither of these courts had any better opportunity to judge Eastman's credibility than we do.

Finally, the state presses an argument that Eastman's testimony was not credible because it relied on "the same type of implausible gun switching and gun juggling that Stumpf told." This, of course, is beside the point. The pertinent fact for Stumpf's due process claim is not whether Eastman's gun-switching story is plausible, but whether the prosecution relied on that story to secure Wesley's conviction. The prosecution found Eastman's testimony credible enough to present the "implausible gun switching" theory to Wesley's jury and obtain his conviction on that theory.

In holding that a constitutional violation occurred in this case, we recognize that at least one circuit has suggested that a due process violation for the use of conflicting theories may be obviated when the second of two inconsistent theories results from the discovery of new evidence. See Thompson, 120 F.3d at 1058 ("when no new significant evidence comes to light a prosecutor cannot, in order to convict two defendants at separate trials, offer inconsistent theories and facts regarding the same crime"). We have no quarrel with this proposition, to the extent that it is meant to acknowledge a state's need to continue to investigate crimes and to present all available evidence in court. However, in this case, although Eastman's testimony did not come to light until after Stumpf had been convicted and sentenced to death, the state had many opportunities to correct its use of conflicting theories. Stumpf, upon learning of the state's reliance on the theory that Wesley was actually the shooter, timely filed a motion to vacate his guilty plea and/or his sentence. The two judges hearing this motion expressed some concern over whether there was evidence that Stumpf was not in fact the shooter, but the state did not take that opportunity to advocate that all the available evidence be presented to the sentencing panel.

* * *

Here, the proper standard of review is whether there is a reasonable probability that the prosecutor's use of inconsistent, irreconcilable theories rendered the conviction unreliable. See, e.g., id. at 706–07; Brady v. Maryland,373 U.S. 83, 83 S.Ct. 1194, 10 L.Ed.2d 215 (1963); Strickland v.

Washington,466 U.S. 668, 694, 104 S.Ct. 2052, 80 L.Ed.2d 674(1984). A "reasonable probability" is a probability sufficient to undermine the outcome and is less than a preponderance of the evidence. *See* Strickland at 694, 104 S.Ct. 2052; Lyons v. Jackson, 299 F.3d 588, 599 (6th Cir.2002).

Measured against this standard, the state's due process violation mandates that both Stumpf's plea and his sentence be set aside. First, there is a reasonable probability that, had the prosecution not pursued conflicting theories concerning who was the actual shooter, Stumpf either would not have pleaded guilty or the three-judge panel would not have found a factual basis for the specific intent element of aggravated murder. Second, and perhaps more likely, there is a reasonable probability that, had the prosecution not pursued inconsistent theories, Stumpf would not have been sentenced to death.

... The prosecution offered virtually no evidence regarding intent other than its contention that Stumpf shot Mrs. Stout. Had the prosecution's alternate theory been heard by the three-judge panel, there is a reasonable probability that it would have found Stumpf guilty of something less than aggravated murder.

* * *

... We REVERSE the district court's decision and REMAND this case to the district court with instructions to issue the writ of habeas corpus in the petitioner's favor, unless the state elects to retry him within 90 days of the date of entry of the conditional writ.

■ BOGGS, CHIEF JUDGE, dissenting.

* * *

... The majority cites three cases from other circuits to buttress its theory that Ohio's prosecution of Wesley, which took place in April 1985, some seven months after Stumpf pleaded guilty and was sentenced to death, somehow violates Stumpf's due process rights. None of the three are germane to this case.

In Thompson v. Calderon, a celebrated California death penalty case, the court vacated a death sentence because the prosecutor presented two mutually incompatible theories for the rape-murder during contemporaneous trials of two defendants, Thompson and Leitch. Thompson v. Calderon, 120 F.3d 1045 (9th Cir.1997) (en banc) (plurality), vacated on other grounds, 523 U.S. 538, 118 S.Ct. 1489, 140 L.Ed.2d 728 (1998). During the pre-trial proceedings for both men, and in Leitch's trial, the prosecutor's theory was that Leitch killed the victim, his girlfriend, because he wanted to get back together with his ex-wife; Thompson assisted him in the crime. In Thompson's trial, however, the prosecutor argued that Thompson had raped the victim and then killed her to cover up his act. He presented different jail house informants at each trial to bolster each contradictory theory. The Ninth Circuit held that this shift in arguments violated a prosecutor's duty to discover the truth and that he was improperly trying to secure convictions for their own sake. Thompson, 120 F.3d at 1058–59.... It also found that Thompson, who was tried first, was prejudiced due that the fact that "[o]nly in Thompson's trial did the prosecutor change the theory and the arguments [from those presented in the pre-trial hearing], and offer facts that directly conflicted with the underlying premise of the charges he brought.'' Thompson, 120 F.3d at 1059.

Distinguishing Thompson from the case before us is not difficult, however. First of all, the prosecutor in Thompson pursued the two mutually incompatible theories of the murder at contemporaneous trials after joint pre-trial proceedings, and deliberately chose witnesses who would tell the conflicting story that he needed to convict each defendant. Knowingly putting on false evidence is prosecutorial misconduct that violates the Due Process Clause. Napue v. Illinois, 360 U.S. 264, 269, 79 S.Ct. 1173, 3 L.Ed.2d 1217 (1959). Nothing in this case indicates that the prosecutors deliberately presented false evidence: Stumpf pleaded guilty to aggravated murder with the specification of killing a witness and attempted aggravated murder with a firearm. The State had every reason to believe his over-all admission of responsibility. It was under no obligation, however, to accept at face value his assertion that he did not actually pull the trigger, especially in light of contradictory forensic evidence, such as the fact that a .25–caliber weapon killed Mrs. Stout, the same caliber as Stumpf's gun.

Nor did the prosecutor in Thompson collect new evidence between trials; he simply manipulated the facts that he had. In contrast, Wesley's trial took place seven months after Stumpf pleaded guilty, during which time informant Eastman told prosecutors that Wesley confessed that he murdered Mrs. Stout. However, Wesley denied having confessed to Eastman, and the forensic evidence suggested that Eastman's statement was not airtight. A cursory comparison of the facts to those in Thompson therefore reveals that the California case has little application to our case.

In Drake v. Kemp, an Eleventh Circuit case, the majority remanded for a new trial because the burden of proof was improperly shifted to the defendant and the prosecutor violated the defendant's rights during his closing arguments in the sentencing phase. Drake v. Kemp, 762 F.2d 1449 (11th Cir.1985) (en banc). A single concurring judge argued that Drake's Fourteenth Amendment rights had been violated. The prosecutor, in trials that were a year apart, argued in one instance that a co-defendant must have committed the murder alone and, after having secured a conviction, argued that same person was not strong enough to commit the crime, and therefore Drake must have helped. The concurring judge concluded that it "seems inescapable that the prosecutor obtained Henry Drake's conviction through the use of testimony he did not believe; bringing this case under the logical if not actual factual framework of . . . Napue.'' Drake, 762 F.2d at 1479 (Clark, J. specially concurring). Drake therefore does not further Stumpf's case either: a concurring opinion that turns on the prosecutor's inferred knowledge that he was presenting false evidence does not comport with the facts in this case.

The last case cited by the majority, Smith v. Groose, 205 F.3d 1045 (8th Cir. 2000), is equally unconvincing. That case involved two groups of robbers, the first of which, when preparing to burglarize a house, discovered the second already in the process of stealing the homeowner's possessions. The two groups joined forces, and at some point during the crime the homeowners were murdered. The leader of the first group, Anthony Lytle, provided varying accounts of what happened, alternately claiming that the head of the second group, Michael Cunningham, killed the couple and that one of his (Lytle's) cohorts, James Bowman, was the murderer. The state convicted Jon Keith Smith, another member of Lytle's group, for felony-murder based on his association with purported fellow gang member Bowman, who was argued to be the actual killer. Four months later, the state then successfully prosecuted Cunningham for the same murders, based on Lytle's other story that Cunningham had already killed the couple when Lytle and his friends entered the house.

The Eighth Circuit ultimately granted Smith a writ of habeas corpus because the state's prosecution of Cunningham violated Smith's due process rights. Again, the crux of the case was the deliberate presentation of false evidence: "In short, what the State claimed to be true in Smith's case it rejected in Cunningham's case, and vice versa." Only a showing of this kind of prosecutorial misconduct could support a claim, dubious as it might be, that Stumpf's constitutional rights were retroactively violated.

Although this court mentions the prosecution's knowledge of Eastman's subsequent statement concerning Wesley's alleged confession to being Mrs. Stout's killer, the court's decision does not rest on this knowledge. It is undisputed that the prosecution did not know of Eastman's statement at the time of Stumpf's conviction and sentencing. Nothing indicates that the prosecution cherry-picked facts in order to confirm Stumpf's guilty plea in the evidentiary hearing. The majority does not argue that the prosecution was under any obligation to confess error in Stumpf's post-conviction proceedings or appeals, nor even to bring Eastman's statement to Stumpf's attention. There is simply no prosecutorial misconduct in this case that could retroactively implicate Stumpf's due process rights.

Groose does not "hold that prosecutors must present precisely the same evidence and theories in trials for different defendants. Rather [it] hold[s] only that the use of inherently factually contradictory theories violates principles of due process."

Far more instructive is the Ninth Circuit's quite recent decision in Shaw v. Terhune, 353 F.3d 697 (9th Cir.2003). The court held that imposing sentence enhancements on two defendants for personal use of a firearm during an attempted robbery and assault on a restaurant manager was not a violation of due process, although the testimony clearly indicated that only one perpetrator had held a gun to the manager's head. When the first defendant, Shaw, learned of the conviction and sentence of his accomplice three years later, he filed a habeas petition, citing the California Court of Appeals decision upholding Watts's sentence which stated: "Indeed, the evidence adduced at trial, which presumably was available to the prosecutor prior to trial, tends to support the conclusion that the jury in [Shaw's] trial was mistaken." People v. Watts, 76 Cal.App.4th 1250, 1259–61, 91 Cal.Rptr.2d 1 (1999).

However, the Shaw court distinguished its case from Thompson, pointing to the fact that the prosecutor did not manipulate evidence—the same crucial distinction that is present in our case. Ambiguous evidence is not false evidence; "regrettable" tactics are not necessarily unconstitutional.

The fact of the matter is that no one but Wesley and Stumpf know who shot Mrs. Stout. The State is entitled to put on the available evidence to convince the finder of fact of guilt. As long as it does so in a good faith manner, without manipulating or selecting out critical evidence, due process is not violated.

The Shaw court also speculated that if there were a constitutional violation, that Watts, the second defendant, rather than Shaw, would be the one who could argue the point. Similarly, I could understand a court accepting Wesley's claim that the prosecution could not honestly present evidence in *his* case that contradicted what the government had relied upon previously (a type of "prosecutorial estoppel"), or even that it could not present evidence that contradicted a position it was taking elsewhere. However, none of those theories can retroactively render unfair the fundamentally fair proceedings that Stumpf received.

Having indicated that I believe it is logically impossible for Stumpf's claim to succeed under these circumstances, I touch only lightly on the court's resolution of the question of "whether there is a reasonable probability that the prosecutor's use of inconsistent, irreconcilable theories rendered the conviction unreliable." Nothing that occurred in Stumpf's proceeding rendered the conviction unreliable. At most, the *existence* of Eastman's statement could be argued to have rendered the conviction unreliable, but then our analysis would simply be that of any newly discovered evidence, which proceeds against a more difficult background and which the court does not undertake. United States v. O'Dell, 805 F.2d 637, 640 (6th Cir.1986) ("Motions for anew trial based on newly discovered evidence are disfavored."); see, e.g., Herrera v. Collins, 506 U.S. 390, 400, 113 S.Ct. 853, 122 L.Ed.2d 203 (1993) (stating the rule that habeas relief is not the proper remedy for a claim of judicial error based on newly discovered evidence, absent some constitutional flaw in the trial proceedings). It would indeed be bizarre if Eastman's statement could not undermine Stumpf's conviction by its own force, but introducing it into another proceeding could do so. Following our court's decision, a prosecutor faced with the same dilemma in the future would be well advised not only to eschew reliance upon such potentially contradictory evidence in later proceedings, but presumably prevent any other prosecutor from doing so. He or she might even be forced deceitfully to disclaim a belief that a jury was entitled to hear such evidence. In sum, whatever the result might be were Wesley bringing the claim, I cannot agree to the principle of retroactive unconstitutionality propounded in this case.

* * *

CHAPTER 21

SENTENCING

B. SENTENCING PROCEDURES

1. BURDEN OF PROOF

Page 1629, add prior to McMillan v. Pennsylvania (New Main Case)

Blakely v. Washington

Supreme Court of the United States, 2004.
___ U.S. ___, 124 S.Ct. 2531.

* * *

■ JUSTICE SCALIA delivered the opinion of the Court.

Sentence raised on court finding of "deliberate cruelty" → 6th Amendment – right to jury trial

Petitioner Ralph Howard Blakely, Jr., pleaded guilty to the kidnaping of his estranged wife. The facts admitted in his plea, standing alone, supported a maximum sentence of 53 months. Pursuant to state law, the court imposed an "exceptional" sentence of 90 months after making a judicial determination that he had acted with "deliberate cruelty." We consider whether this violated petitioner's *Sixth Amendment* right to trial by jury.

Petitioner married his wife Yolanda in 1973. He was evidently a difficult man to live with, having been diagnosed at various times with psychological and personality disorders including paranoid schizophrenia. His wife ultimately filed for divorce. In 1998, he abducted her from their orchard home in Grant County, Washington, binding her with duct tape and forcing her at knifepoint into a wooden box in the bed of his pickup truck. In the process, he implored her to dismiss the divorce suit and related trust proceedings.

When the couple's 13-year-old son Ralphy returned home from school, petitioner ordered him to follow in another car, threatening to harm Yolanda with a shotgun if he did not do so. Ralphy escaped and sought help when they stopped at a gas station, but petitioner continued on with Yolanda to a friend's house in Montana. He was finally arrested after the friend called the police.

* * *

The case then proceeded to sentencing. In Washington, second-degree kidnaping is a class B felony § 9A.40.030(3). State law provides that "no person convicted of a [class B] felony shall be punished by confinement . . . exceeding . . . a term of ten years." *§ 9A.20.021(1)(b)*. Other provisions of state law, however, further limit the range of sentences a judge may impose. *Washington's Sentencing Reform Act* specifies, for petitioner's offense of second-degree kidnaping with a firearm, a "standard range" of 49 to 53 months.... A judge may impose a sentence above the standard range if he finds "substantial and compelling reasons justifying an exceptional sentence." *The Act* lists aggravating factors that justify such a departure, which it recites to be illustrative rather than exhaustive. Nevertheless, "[a] reason offered to justify an exceptional sentence can be considered only if it takes into account factors other than those which are used in computing the standard range sentence for the offense." *State v. Gore, 143 Wn. 2d 288, 315–316, 21 P. 3d 262, 277 (2001).* When a judge imposes an exceptional sentence, he must set forth findings of fact and conclusions of law supporting it. A reviewing court will reverse the sentence if it finds that "under a clearly erroneous standard there is insufficient evidence in the record to support the reasons for imposing an exceptional sentence." *Gore, supra, at 315, 21 P. 3d, at 277.*

Pursuant to the plea agreement, the State recommended a sentence within the standard range of 49 to 53 months. After hearing Yolanda's description of the kidnaping, however, the judge rejected the State's recommendation and imposed an exceptional sentence of 90 months—37 months beyond the standard maximum. He justified the sentence on the ground that petitioner had acted with "deliberate cruelty," a statutorily enumerated ground for departure in domestic-violence cases.

Faced with an unexpected increase of more than three years in his sentence, petitioner objected. The judge accordingly conducted a 3–day bench hearing featuring testimony from petitioner, Yolanda, Ralphy, a police officer, and medical experts. After the hearing, he issued 32 findings of fact, concluding:

> "The defendant's motivation to commit kidnapping was complex, contributed to by his mental condition and personality disorders, the pressures of the divorce litigation, the impending trust litigation trial and anger over his troubled interpersonal relationships with his spouse and children. While he misguidedly intended to forcefully reunite his family, his attempt to do so was subservient to his desire to terminate lawsuits and modify title ownerships to his benefit.

"The defendant's methods were more homogeneous than his motive. He used stealth and surprise, and took advantage of the victim's isolation. He immediately employed physical violence, restrained the victim with tape, and threatened her with injury and death to herself and others. He immediately coerced the victim into providing information by the threatening application of a knife. He violated a subsisting restraining order." App. 48–49.

The judge adhered to his initial determination of deliberate cruelty.

Petitioner appealed, arguing that this sentencing procedure deprived him of his federal constitutional right to have a jury determine beyond a reasonable doubt all facts legally essential to his sentence. The State Court of Appeals affirmed.... The Washington Supreme Court denied discretionary review. We granted certiorari.

II

This case requires us to apply the rule we expressed in *Apprendi v. New Jersey, 530 U.S. 466, 490, 147 L. Ed. 2d 435, 120 S. Ct. 2348 (2000)*: "Other than the fact of a prior conviction, any fact that increases the penalty for a crime beyond the prescribed statutory maximum must be submitted to a jury, and proved beyond a reasonable doubt." This rule reflects two longstanding tenets of common-law criminal jurisprudence: that the "truth of every accusation" against a defendant "should afterwards be confirmed by the unanimous suffrage of twelve of his equals and neighbours," 4 W. Blackstone, Commentaries on the Laws of England 343 (1769). . . .

Apprendi involved a New Jersey hate-crime statute that authorized a 20–year sentence, despite the usual 10–year maximum, if the judge found the crime to have been committed " 'with a purpose to intimidate . . . because of race, color, gender, handicap, religion, sexual orientation or ethnicity.' " In *Ring v. Arizona, 536 U.S. 584, 592–593, 153 L. Ed. 2d 556, 122 S. Ct. 2428* (2002), we applied *Apprendi* to an Arizona law that authorized the death penalty if the judge found one of ten aggravating factors. In each case, we concluded that the defendant's constitutional rights had been violated because the judge had imposed a sentence greater than the maximum he could have imposed under state law without the challenged factual finding. . . .

. . . The State contends that there was no *Apprendi* violation because the relevant "statutory maximum" is not 53 months, but the 10–year maximum for class B felonies. It observes that no exceptional sentence may exceed that limit. Our precedents make clear, however, that the "statutory maximum" for *Apprendi* purposes is the maximum sentence a judge may impose *solely on the basis of the facts reflected in the jury verdict or admitted by the defendant*. See *Ring, supra, at 602, 153 L. Ed. 2d 556, 122 S. Ct. 2428* (" 'the maximum he would receive if punished according to the facts reflected in the jury verdict alone' " (quoting *Apprendi, supra, at 483*.) In other words, the relevant "statutory maximum" is not the maximum sentence a judge may impose after finding additional facts, but the maximum he may impose *without* any additional findings. When a judge inflicts punishment that the jury's verdict alone does not allow, the jury has not found all the facts "which the law makes essential to the punishment," 1 J. Bishop, Criminal Procedure, (2d Ed 1872), § 87, at 55, and the judge exceeds his proper authority.

The judge in this case could not have imposed the exceptional 90–month sentence solely on the basis of the facts admitted in the guilty plea. Those facts alone were insufficient because, as the Washington Supreme Court has explained, "[a] reason offered to justify an exceptional sentence can be considered only if it takes into account factors other than those which are used in computing the standard range sentence for the offense," *Gore, 143 Wash. 2d, at 315–316, 21 P. 3d, at 277*, which in this case included the elements of second-degree kidnaping and the use of a firearm. Had the judge imposed the 90–month sentence solely on the basis of the plea, he would have been reversed. The "maximum sentence" is no more 10 years here than it was 20 years in *Apprendi* (because that is what the judge could have imposed upon finding a hate crime) or death in *Ring* (because that is what the judge could have imposed upon finding an aggravator).

The State defends the sentence by drawing an analogy to those we upheld in *McMillan v. Pennsylvania, 477 U.S. 79, 91 L. Ed. 2d 67, 106 S. Ct. 2411 (1986)*, and *Williams v. New York, 337 U.S. 241, 93 L. Ed. 1337, 69 S. Ct. 1079 (1949)*. Neither case is on point. *McMillan* involved a sentencing scheme that imposed a statutory *minimum* if a judge found a particular fact. *477 U.S., at 81, 91 L. Ed. 2d 67, 106 S. Ct. 2411*. We specifically noted that the statute "does not authorize a sentence in excess of that otherwise allowed for [the underlying] offense." *Williams* involved an indeterminate-sentencing regime that allowed a judge (but did not compel him) to rely on facts outside the trial record in determining whether to sentence a defendant to death. The judge could have "sentenced [the defendant] to death giving no reason at all." *Id., at 252, 93 L. Ed. 1337, 69 S. Ct. 1079*. Thus, neither case involved a sentence greater than what state law authorized on the basis of the verdict alone.

* * *

Because the State's sentencing procedure did not comply with the *Sixth Amendment*, petitioner's sentence is invalid.

III

Our commitment to *Apprendi* in this context reflects not just respect for longstanding precedent, but the need to give intelligible content to the right of jury trial. That right is no mere procedural formality, but a fundamental reservation of power in our constitutional structure. Just as suffrage ensures the people's ultimate control in the legislative and executive branches, jury trial is meant to ensure their control in the judiciary. See Letter XV by the Federal Farmer (Jan. 18, 1788), reprinted in 2 The Complete Anti–Federalist 315, 320 (H. Storing ed. 1981) (describing the jury as "securing to the people at large, their just and rightful controul in the judicial department"); John Adams, Diary Entry (Feb. 12, 1771), reprinted in 2 Works of John Adams 252, 253 (C. Adams ed. 1850) ("The common people, should have as complete a control . . . in every judgment of a court of judicature" as in the legislature); Letter from Thomas Jefferson to the Abbe Arnoux (July 19, 1789), reprinted in 15 Papers of Thomas Jefferson 282, 283 (J. Boyd ed. 1958) ("Were I called upon to decide whether the people had best be omitted in the Legislative or Judiciary department, I would say it is better to leave them out of the Legislative"); *Jones v. United States, 526 U.S. 227, 244–248, 143 L. Ed. 2d 311, 119 S. Ct. 1215 (1999)*. *Apprendi* carries out this design by ensuring that the judge's authority to sentence derives wholly from the jury's verdict. Without that restriction, the jury would not exercise the control that the Framers intended.

Those who would reject *Apprendi* are resigned to one of two alternatives. The first is that the jury need only find whatever facts the legislature chooses to label elements of the crime, and that those it labels sentencing factors—no matter how much they may increase the punishment—may be found by the judge. This would mean, for example, that a judge could sentence a man for committing murder even if the jury convicted him only of illegally possessing the firearm used to commit it—or of making an illegal lane change while fleeing the death scene. Not even *Apprendi*'s critics would advocate this absurd result. Cf. *530 U.S., at 552–553, 147 L. Ed. 2d 435, 120 S. Ct. 2348* (O'CONNOR, J., dissenting). The jury could not function as circuitbreaker in the State's machinery of justice if it were relegated to making a determination that the defendant at some point did something wrong, a mere preliminary to a judicial inquisition into the facts of the crime the State *actually* seeks to punish.

The second alternative is that legislatures may establish legally essential sentencing factors *within limits*—limits crossed when, perhaps, the sentencing factor is a "tail which wags the dog of the substantive offense." *McMillan, 477 U.S., at 88, 91 L. Ed. 2d 67, 106 S. Ct. 2411.* What this means in operation is that the law must not go *too far*—it must not exceed the judicial estimation of the proper role of the judge.

The subjectivity of this standard is obvious. Petitioner argued below that second-degree kidnaping with deliberate cruelty was essentially the same as first-degree kidnaping, the very charge he had avoided by pleading to a lesser offense. The court conceded this might be so but held it irrelevant. Petitioner's 90–month sentence exceeded the 53–month standard maximum by almost 70%; the Washington Supreme Court in other cases has upheld exceptional sentences 15 times the standard maximum. See *State v. Oxborrow, 106 Wn. 2d 525, 528, 533, 723 P.2d 1123, 1125, 1128 (1986)* (15–year exceptional sentence; 1–year standard maximum sentence); *State v. Branch, 129 Wn. 2d 635, 650, 919 P.2d 1228, 1235 (1996)* (4–year exceptional sentence; 3–month standard maximum sentence). Did the court go *too far* in any of these cases? There is no answer that legal analysis can provide. With *too far* as the yardstick, it is always possible to disagree with such judgments and never to refute them.

Another example of conversion from separate crime to sentence enhancement that JUSTICE O'CONNOR evidently does not consider going "too far" is the obstruction-of-justice enhancement, see *post*, at 6–7. Why perjury during trial should be grounds for a judicial sentence enhancement on the underlying offense, rather than an entirely separate offense to be found by a jury beyond a reasonable doubt (as it has been for centuries, see 4 W. Blackstone, Commentaries on the Laws of England 136–138 (1769)), is unclear.

Whether the *Sixth Amendment* incorporates this manipulable standard rather than *Apprendi*'s bright-line rule depends on the plausibility of the claim that the Framers would have left definition of the scope of jury power up to judges' intuitive sense of how far is *too far*. We think that claim not plausible at all, because the very reason the Framers put a jury-trial guarantee in the Constitution is that they were unwilling to trust government to mark out the role of the jury.

IV

. . . This case is not about whether determinate sentencing is constitutional, only about how it can be implemented in a way that respects the

Sixth Amendment. Several policies prompted Washington's adoption of determinate sentencing, including proportionality to the gravity of the offense and parity among defendants. See *Wash. Rev. Code Ann. § 9.94A.010* (2000). Nothing we have said impugns those salutary objectives.

Justice O'Connor argues that, because determinate sentencing schemes involving judicial factfinding entail less judicial discretion than indeterminate schemes, the constitutionality of the latter implies the constitutionality of the former. This argument is flawed on a number of levels. First, the *Sixth Amendment* by its terms is not a limitation on judicial power, but a reservation of jury power. It limits judicial power only to the extent that the claimed judicial power infringes on the province of the jury. Indeterminate sentencing does not do so. It increases judicial discretion, to be sure, but not at the expense of the jury's traditional function of finding the facts essential to lawful imposition of the penalty. Of course indeterminate schemes involve judicial factfinding, in that a judge (like a parole board) may implicitly rule on those facts he deems important to the exercise of his sentencing discretion. But the facts do not pertain to whether the defendant has a legal *right* to a lesser sentence—and that makes all the difference insofar as judicial impingement upon the traditional role of the jury is concerned. In a system that says the judge may punish burglary with 10 to 40 years, every burglar knows he is risking 40 years in jail. In a system that punishes burglary with a 10–year sentence, with another 30 added for use of a gun, the burglar who enters a home unarmed is *entitled* to no more than a 10–year sentence—and by reason of the *Sixth Amendment* the facts bearing upon that entitlement must be found by a jury.

But even assuming that restraint of judicial power unrelated to the jury's role is a *Sixth Amendment* objective, it is far from clear that *Apprendi* disserves that goal. Determinate judicial-factfinding schemes entail less judicial power than indeterminate schemes, but more judicial power than determinate *jury*-factfinding schemes. Whether *Apprendi* increases judicial power overall depends on what States with determinate judicial-factfinding schemes would do, given the choice between the two alternatives. Justice O'Connor simply assumes that the net effect will favor judges, but she has no empirical basis for that prediction. Indeed, what evidence we have points exactly the other way: When the Kansas Supreme Court found *Apprendi* infirmities in that State's determinate-sentencing regime in *State v. Gould, 271 Kan. 394, 404–414, 23 P. 3d 801, 809–814 (2001)*, the legislature responded not by reestablishing indeterminate sentencing but by applying *Apprendi*'s requirements to its current regime. See *Kan. Stat. Ann. § 21–4718* (2003 Cum. Supp.).... The result was less, not more, judicial power.

Justice Breyer argues that *Apprendi* works to the detriment of criminal defendants who plead guilty by depriving them of the opportunity to argue sentencing factors to a judge. But nothing prevents a defendant from waiving his *Apprendi* rights. When a defendant pleads guilty, the State is free to seek judicial sentence enhancements so long as the defendant either stipulates to the relevant facts or consents to judicial factfinding. If appropriate waivers are procured, States may continue to offer judicial factfinding as a matter of course to all defendants who plead guilty. Even a defendant who stands trial may consent to judicial factfinding as to sentence enhancements, which may well be in his interest if relevant evidence would prejudice him at trial. We do not understand how *Apprendi* can possibly work to the detriment of those who are free, if they think its costs outweigh its benefits, to render it inapplicable.

Nor do we see any merit to JUSTICE BREYER's contention that *Apprendi* is unfair to criminal defendants because, if States respond by enacting "17–element robbery crimes," prosecutors will have more elements with which to bargain.... Bargaining already exists with regard to sentencing factors because defendants can either stipulate or contest the facts that make them applicable. If there is any difference between bargaining over sentencing factors and bargaining over elements, the latter probably favors the defendant. Every new element that a prosecutor can threaten to charge is also an element that a defendant can threaten to contest at trial and make the prosecutor prove beyond a reasonable doubt. Moreover, given the sprawling scope of most criminal codes, and the power to affect sentences by making (even nonbinding) sentencing recommendations, there is already no shortage of *in terrorem* tools at prosecutors' disposal.... Any evaluation of *Apprendi*'s "fairness" to criminal defendants must compare it with the regime it replaced, in which a defendant, with no warning in either his indictment or plea, would routinely see his maximum potential sentence balloon from as little as five years to as much as life imprisonment, see *21 U.S.C. § § 841(b)(1)(A), (D)*,[2] based not on facts proved to his peers beyond a reasonable doubt, but on facts extracted after trial from a report compiled by a probation officer who the judge thinks more likely got it right than got it wrong. We can conceive of no measure of fairness that would find more fault in the utterly speculative bargaining effects JUSTICE BREYER identifies than in the regime he champions. Suffice it to say that, if such a measure exists, it is not the one the Framers left us with.

* * *

JUSTICE BREYER also claims that *Apprendi* will attenuate the connection between "real criminal conduct and real punishment" by encouraging plea bargaining and by restricting alternatives to adversarial factfinding. The short answer to the former point (even assuming the questionable premise that *Apprendi* does encourage plea bargaining), is that the *Sixth Amendment* was not written for the benefit of those who choose to forgo its protection. It guarantees the *right* to jury trial. It does not guarantee that a particular number of jury trials will actually take place. That more defendants elect to waive that right (because, for example, government at the

2. To be sure, JUSTICE BREYER and the other dissenters would forbid those increases of sentence that violate the constitutional principle that tail shall not wag dog. The source of this principle is entirely unclear. Its precise effect, if precise effect it has, is presumably to require that the ratio of sentencing-factor add-on to basic criminal sentence be no greater than the ratio of caudal vertebrae to body in the breed of canine with the longest tail. Or perhaps no greater than the average such ratio for all breeds. Or perhaps the median. Regrettably, *Apprendi* has prevented full development of this line of jurisprudence.

moment is not particularly oppressive) does not prove that a constitutional provision guaranteeing *availability* of that option is disserved.

JUSTICE BREYER's more general argument—that *Apprendi* undermines alternatives to adversarial factfinding—is not so much a criticism of *Apprendi* as an assault on jury trial generally. His esteem for "non-adversarial" truth-seeking processes, supports just as well an argument against either. Our Constitution and the common-law traditions it entrenches, however, do not admit the contention that facts are better discovered by judicial inquisition than by adversarial testing before a jury. See 3 Blackstone, Commentaries, at 373–374, 379–381. JUSTICE BREYER may be convinced of the equity of the regime he favors, but his views are not the ones we are bound to uphold.

Ultimately, our decision cannot turn on whether or to what degree trial by jury impairs the efficiency or fairness of criminal justice. One can certainly argue that both these values would be better served by leaving justice entirely in the hands of professionals; many nations of the world, particularly those following civil-law traditions, take just that course. There is not one shred of doubt, however, about the Framers' paradigm for criminal justice: not the civil-law ideal of administrative perfection, but the common-law ideal of limited state power accomplished by strict division of authority between judge and jury. As *Apprendi* held, every defendant has the *right* to insist that the prosecutor prove to a jury all facts legally essential to the punishment. Under the dissenters' alternative, he has no such right. That should be the end of the matter.

* * *

Petitioner was sentenced to prison for more than three years beyond what the law allowed for the crime to which he confessed, on the basis of a disputed finding that he had acted with "deliberate cruelty." The Framers would not have thought it too much to demand that, before depriving a man of three more years of his liberty, the State should suffer the modest inconvenience of submitting its accusation to "the unanimous suffrage of twelve of his equals and neighbours," rather than a lone employee of the State.

The judgment of the Washington Court of Appeals is reversed, and the case is remanded for further proceedings not inconsistent with this opinion.

* * *

■ JUSTICE O'CONNOR, with whom JUSTICE BREYER joins, and with whom THE CHIEF JUSTICE and JUSTICE KENNEDY join as to all but Part IV–B, dissenting.

The legacy of today's opinion, whether intended or not, will be the consolidation of sentencing power in the State and Federal Judiciaries. The Court says to Congress and state legislatures: If you want to constrain the sentencing discretion of judges and bring some uniformity to sentencing, it will cost you—dearly. Congress and States, faced with the burdens imposed by the extension of *Apprendi* to the present context, will either trim or eliminate altogether their sentencing guidelines schemes and, with them, 20 years of sentencing reform. It is thus of little moment that the majority does not expressly declare guidelines schemes unconstitutional, for, as residents of "*Apprendi*-land" are fond of saying, "the relevant inquiry is one not of form, but of effect." *Apprendi v. New Jersey, (2000)*. The "effect" of today's decision will be greater judicial discretion and less uniformity in sentencing. Because I find it implausible that the Framers would have considered such a result to be required by the *Due Process Clause* or the *Sixth Amendment*, and because the practical consequences of today's decision may be disastrous, I respectfully dissent.

I

One need look no further than the history leading up to and following the enactment of Washington's guidelines scheme to appreciate the damage that today's decision will cause. Prior to 1981, Washington, like most other States and the Federal Government, employed an indeterminate sentencing scheme. Washington's criminal code separated all felonies into three broad categories: "class A," carrying a sentence of 20 years to life; "class B," carrying a sentence of 0 to 10 years; and "class C," carrying a sentence of 0 to 5 years. Sentencing judges, in conjunction with parole boards, had virtually unfettered discretion to sentence defendants to prison terms falling anywhere within the statutory range, including probation—*i.e.*, no jail sentence at all....

This system of unguided discretion inevitably resulted in severe disparities in sentences received and served by defendants committing the same offense and having similar criminal histories.... Indeed, rather than reflect legally relevant criteria, these disparities too often were correlated with constitutionally suspect variables such as race. See also Breyer, The Federal Sentencing Guidelines and Key Compromises Upon Which They Rest, *17 Hofstra L. Rev. 1, 5 (1988)* (elimination of racial disparity one reason behind Congress' creation of the Federal Sentencing Commission).

Indeterminate Sentencing vs. Determinate Sentencing.

To counteract these trends, the state legislature passed the *Sentencing Reform Act of 1981*.... The Act neither increased any of the statutory sentencing ranges for the three types of felonies (though it did eliminate the statutory mandatory minimum for class A felonies), nor reclassified any substantive offenses. It merely placed meaningful constraints on discretion to sentence offenders within the statutory ranges, and eliminated parole. There is thus no evidence that the legislature was attempting to manipulate the statutory elements of criminal offenses or to circumvent the procedural protections of the *Bill of Rights*. Rather, lawmakers were trying to bring some much-needed uniformity, transparency, and accountability to an otherwise " 'labyrinthine' sentencing and corrections system that 'lacked any principle except unguided discretion.' " (quoting F. Zimring, Making the Punishment Fit the Crime: A Consumers' Guide to Sentencing Reform, Occasional Paper No. 12, p. 6 (1977).

Far from disregarding principles of due process and the jury trial right, as the majority today suggests, Washington's reform has served them. Before passage of the Act, a defendant charged with second degree kidnapping, like petitioner, had no idea whether he would receive a 10–year sentence or probation. The ultimate sentencing determination could turn as much on the idiosyncracies of a particular judge as on the specifics of the defendant's crime or background. A defendant did not know what facts, if any, about his offense or his history would be considered relevant by the sentencing judge or by the parole board. After passage of the Act, a defendant charged with second degree kidnaping knows what his presumptive sentence will be; he has a good idea of the types of factors that a sentencing judge can and will consider when deciding whether to sentence him outside that range; he is guaranteed meaningful appellate review to protect against an arbitrary sentence. . . . Criminal defendants still face the same statutory maximum sentences, but they now at least know, much more than before, the real consequences of their actions.

Washington's move to a system of guided discretion has served equal protection principles as well. Over the past 20 years, there has been a substantial reduction in racial disparity in sentencing across the State. . . .

The majority does not, because it cannot, disagree that determinate sentencing schemes, like Washington's, serve important constitutional values. Thus, the majority says: "this case is not about whether determinate sentencing is constitutional, only about how it can be implemented in a way that respects the *Sixth Amendment*." But extension of *Apprendi* to the present context will impose significant costs on a legislature's determination that a particular fact, not historically an element, warrants a higher sentence. While not a constitutional prohibition on guidelines schemes, the majority's decision today exacts a substantial constitutional tax.

The costs are substantial and real. Under the majority's approach, any fact that increases the upper bound on a judge's sentencing discretion is an element of the offense. Thus, facts that historically have been taken into account by sentencing judges to assess a sentence within a broad range—such as drug quantity, role in the offense, risk of bodily harm—all must now be charged in an indictment and submitted to a jury, *In re Winship, 397 U.S. 358, 25 L. Ed. 2d 368, 90 S. Ct. 1068 (1970)*, simply because it is the legislature, rather than the judge, that constrains the extent to which such facts may be used to impose a sentence within a pre-existing statutory range.

While that alone is enough to threaten the continued use of sentencing guidelines schemes, there are additional costs. For example, a legislature might rightly think that some factors bearing on sentencing, such as prior bad acts or criminal history, should not be considered in a jury's determination of a defendant's guilt—such "character evidence" has traditionally been off limits during the guilt phase of criminal proceedings because of its tendency to inflame the passions of the jury. See, *e.g.*, *Fed. Rule Evid. 404*; 1 E. Imwinkelried, P. Giannelli, F. Gilligan, & F. Leaderer, Courtroom Criminal Evidence 285 (3d ed. 1998). If a legislature desires uniform consideration of such factors at sentencing, but does not want them to impact a jury's initial determination of guilt, the State may have to bear the additional expense of a separate, full-blown jury trial during the penalty phase proceeding.

Some facts that bear on sentencing either will not be discovered, or are not discoverable, prior to trial. For instance, a legislature might desire that defendants who act in an obstructive manner during trial or post-trial proceedings receive a greater sentence than defendants who do not. See, *e.g.*, United States Sentencing Commission, Guidelines Manual, § 3C1.1 (Nov. 2003) (hereinafter USSG) (2–point increase in offense level for obstruction of justice). In such cases, the violation arises too late for the State to provide notice to the defendant or to argue the facts to the jury. A State wanting to make such facts relevant at sentencing must now either vest sufficient discretion in the judge to account for them *or* bring a separate criminal prosecution for obstruction of justice or perjury. And, the latter option is available only to the extent that a defendant's obstructive behavior is so severe as to constitute an already-existing separate offense, unless the legislature is willing to undertake the unlikely expense of criminalizing relatively minor obstructive behavior.

Likewise, not all facts that historically have been relevant to sentencing always will be known prior to trial. For instance, trial or sentencing proceedings of a drug distribution defendant might reveal that he sold primarily to children. Under the majority's approach, a State wishing such a revelation to result in a higher sentence within a pre-existing statutory range either must vest judges with sufficient discretion to account for it (and trust that they exercise that discretion) *or* bring a separate criminal prosecution. Indeed, the latter choice might not be available—a separate prosecution, if it is for an aggravated offense, likely would be barred altogether by the *Double Jeopardy Clause. Blockburger v. United States, 284 U.S. 299, 76 L. Ed. 306, 52 S. Ct. 180 (1932)* (cannot prosecute for separate offense unless the two offenses both have at least one element that the other does not).

The majority may be correct that States and the Federal Government will be willing to bear some of these costs. But simple economics dictate that they will not, and cannot, bear them all. To the extent that they do not, there will be an inevitable increase in judicial discretion with all of its attendant failings. n1

Washington's Sentencing Reform Act did not alter the statutory maximum sentence to which petitioner was exposed.

Petitioner was informed in the charging document, his plea agreement, and during his plea hearing that he faced a potential statutory maximum of 10 years in prison. The guidelines served due process by providing notice to petitioner of the consequences of his acts; they vindicated his jury trial right by informing him of the stakes of risking trial; they served equal protection by ensuring petitioner that invidious characteristics such as race would not impact his sentence.

Given these observations, it is difficult for me to discern what principle besides doctrinaire formalism actually motivates today's decision. The majority chides the *Apprendi* dissenters for preferring a nuanced interpretation of the *Due Process Clause and Sixth Amendment* jury trial guarantee that would generally defer to legislative labels while acknowledging the existence of constitutional constraints—what the majority calls the "the law must not go too far" approach. If indeed the choice is between adopting a balanced case-by-case approach that takes into consideration the values underlying the *Bill of Rights*, as well as the history of a particular sentencing reform law, and adopting a rigid rule that destroys everything in its path, I will choose the former. . . .

But even were one to accept formalism as a principle worth vindicating for its own sake, it would not explain *Apprendi*'s, or today's, result. A rule of deferring to legislative labels has no less formal pedigree. It would be more consistent with our decisions leading up to *Apprendi*, see *Almendarez-Torres v. United States, 523 U.S. 224, 140 L. Ed. 2d 350, 118 S. Ct. 1219 (1998)* (fact of prior conviction not an element of aggravated recidivist offense); *United States v. Watts, 519 U.S. 148, 136 L. Ed. 2d 554, 117 S. Ct. 633 (1997) (per curiam)* (acquittal of offense no bar to consideration of underlying conduct for purposes of guidelines enhancement); *Witte v. United States, 515 U.S. 389, 132 L. Ed. 2d 351, 115 S. Ct. 2199 (1995)* (no double jeopardy bar against consideration of uncharged conduct in imposition of guidelines enhancement); *Walton v. Arizona, 497 U.S. 639, 111 L. Ed. 2d 511, 110 S. Ct. 3047 (1990)* (aggravating factors need not be found by a jury in capital case); *Mistretta v. United States, 488 U.S. 361, 102 L. Ed. 2d 714, 109 S. Ct. 647 (1989)* (Federal Sentencing Guidelines do not violate separation of powers); *McMillan v. Pennsylvania, 477 U.S. 79, 91 L. Ed. 2d 67, 106 S. Ct. 2411 (1986)* (facts increasing mandatory minimum sentence are not necessarily elements); and it would vest primary authority for defining crimes in the political branches, where it belongs. It also would be easier to administer than the majority's rule, inasmuch as courts would not be forced to look behind statutes and regulations to determine whether a particular fact does or does not increase the penalty to which a defendant was exposed.

The majority is correct that rigid adherence to such an approach *could conceivably* produce absurd results, but, as today's decision demonstrates, rigid adherence to the majority's approach *does and will continue* to produce results that disserve the very principles the majority purports to vindicate. The pre-*Apprendi* rule of deference to the legislature retains a built-in political check to prevent lawmakers from shifting the prosecution for crimes to the penalty phase proceedings of lesser included and easier-to-prove offenses—*e.g.*, the majority's hypothesized prosecution of murder in the guise of a traffic offense sentencing proceeding. There is no similar check, however, on application of the majority's " 'any fact that increases the upper bound of judicial discretion' " by courts.

* * *

IV

A

The consequences of today's decision will be as far reaching as they are disturbing. Washington's sentencing system is by no means unique. Numerous other States have enacted guidelines systems, as has the Federal Government. See, *e.g., Alaska Stat. § 12.55.155* (2003); *Ark. Code Ann. § 16–90–804* (Supp. 2003); *Fla. Stat. § 921.0016* (2003); *Kan. Stat. Ann. § 21–4701 et seq.* (2003); *Mich. Comp. Laws Ann. § 769.34* (West Supp. 2004); *Minn. Stat. § 244.10* (2002); *N. C. Gen. Stat. § 15A–1340.16* (Lexis 2003); Ore. Admin. Rule § 213–008–0001 (2003); 204 Pa. Code § 303 *et seq.* (2004), reproduced following *42 Pa. Cons. Stat. Ann. § 9721* (Purden Supp. 2004); *18 U.S.C. § 3553*; *28 U.S.C. § 991 et seq.* Today's decision casts constitutional doubt over them all and, in so doing, threatens an untold number of criminal judgments. Every sentence imposed under such guidelines in cases currently pending on direct appeal is in jeopardy. And, despite the fact that we hold in *Schriro* v. *Summerlin, post,* p. ___, that *Ring* (and *a fortiori Apprendi*) does not apply retroactively on habeas review, all criminal sentences imposed under the federal and state guidelines since *Apprendi* was decided in 2000 arguably remain open to collateral attack....

The practical consequences for trial courts, starting today, will be equally unsettling: How are courts to mete out guidelines sentences? Do courts apply the guidelines as to mitigating factors, but not as to aggravating factors? Do they jettison the guidelines altogether? The Court ignores the havoc it is about to wreak on trial courts across the country.

* * *

What I have feared most has now come to pass: Over 20 years of sentencing reform are all but lost, and tens of thousands of criminal judgments are in jeopardy. *Apprendi, 530 U.S., at 549–559, 147 L. Ed. 2d 435, 120 S. Ct. 2348* (O'CONNOR, J., dissenting); *Ring, 536 U.S., at 619–621, 153 L. Ed. 2d 556, 122 S. Ct. 2428* (O'CONNOR, J., dissenting). I respectfully dissent.

■ JUSTICE KENNEDY, with whom JUSTICE BREYER joins, dissenting.

The majority opinion does considerable damage to our laws and to the administration of the criminal justice system for all the reasons well stated in JUSTICE O'CONNOR'S dissent, plus one more: The Court, in my respectful submission, disregards the fundamental principle under our constitutional system that different branches of government "converse with each other on matters of vital common interest." *Mistretta v. United States, 488 U.S. 361, 408, 102 L. Ed. 2d 714, 109 S. Ct. 647 (1989)*. As the Court in *Mistretta* explained, the Constitution establishes a system of government that presupposes, not just " 'autonomy' " and " 'separateness,' " but also " 'interdependence' " and " 'reciprocity.' " *Id., at 381, 102 L. Ed. 2d 714, 109 S. Ct. 647* (quoting *Youngstown Sheet & Tube Co. v. Sawyer, 343 U.S. 579, 635, 96 L. Ed. 1153, 72 S. Ct. 863, 62 Ohio Law Abs. 417 (1952)* (Jackson, J., concurring)). Constant, constructive discourse between our courts and our legislatures is an integral and admirable part of the constitutional design. Case-by-case judicial determinations often yield intelligible patterns that can be refined by legislatures and codified into statutes or rules as general standards. As these legislative enactments are followed by incremental judicial interpretation, the legislatures may respond again, and the cycle repeats. This recurring dialogue, an essential source for the elaboration and the evolution of the law, is basic constitutional theory in action.

Sentencing guidelines are a prime example of this collaborative process. Dissatisfied with the wide disparity in sentencing, participants in the criminal justice system, including judges, pressed for legislative reforms. In response, legislators drew from these participants' shared experiences and enacted measures to correct the problems, which, as JUSTICE O'CONNOR explains, could sometimes rise to the level of a constitutional injury. As *Mistretta* recognized, this interchange among different actors in the constitutional scheme is consistent with the Constitution's structural protections.

To be sure, this case concerns the work of a state legislature, and not of Congress. If anything, however, this distinction counsels even greater judicial caution. Unlike *Mistretta*, the case here implicates not just the collective wisdom of legislators on the other side of the continuing dialogue over fair sentencing, but also the interest of the States to serve as laboratories for innovation and experiment. See *New State Ice Co. v. Liebmann, 285 U.S. 262, 311, 76 L. Ed. 747, 52 S. Ct. 371 (1932)* (Brandeis, J., dissenting). With no apparent sense of irony that the effect of today's decision is the destruction of a sentencing scheme devised by democratically elected legislators, the majority shuts down alternative, nonjudicial, sources of ideas and experience. It does so under a faintly disguised distrust of judges and their purported usurpation of the jury's function in criminal trials. It tells not only trial judges who have spent years studying the problem but also legislators who have devoted valuable time and resources "calling upon the accumulated wisdom and experience of the Judicial Branch ... on a matter uniquely within the ken of judges," *Mistretta, supra, at 412, 102 L. Ed. 2d 714, 109 S. Ct. 647*, that their efforts and judgments were all for naught. Numerous States that have enacted sentencing guidelines similar to the one in Washington State are now commanded to scrap everything and start over.

* * *

■ JUSTICE BREYER, with whom JUSTICE O'CONNOR joins, dissenting.

The Court makes clear that it means what it said in *Apprendi v. New Jersey, 530 U.S. 466, 147 L. Ed. 2d 435, 120 S. Ct. 2348 (2000).* In its view, the *Sixth Amendment* says that " 'any fact that increases the penalty for a crime beyond the prescribed statutory maximum must be submitted to a jury.' " *Ante,* at 5 (quoting *Apprendi, supra, at 490, 147 L. Ed. 2d 435, 120 S. Ct. 2348*). " 'Prescribed statutory maximum' " means the penalty that the relevant statute authorizes "solely on the basis of the facts reflected in the jury verdict." *Ante,* at 7 (emphasis deleted). Thus, a jury must find, not only the facts that make up the crime of which the offender is charged, but also all (punishment-increasing) facts about the *way* in which the offender carried out that crime.

It is not difficult to understand the impulse that produced this holding. Imagine a classic example—a statute (or mandatory sentencing guideline) that provides a 10–year sentence for ordinary bank robbery, but a 15–year sentence for bank robbery committed with a gun. One might ask why it should matter for jury trial purposes whether the statute (or guideline) labels the gun's presence (a) a *sentencing fact* about the way in which the offender carried out the *lesser* crime of ordinary bank robbery, or (b) a factual *element* of the *greater* crime of bank robbery with a gun? If the *Sixth Amendment* requires a jury finding about the gun in the latter circumstance, why should it not also require a jury to find the same fact in the former circumstance? The two sets of circumstances are functionally identical. In both instances, identical punishment follows from identical factual findings (related to, *e.g.*, a bank, a taking, a thing-of-value, force or threat of force, and a gun). The only difference between the two circumstances concerns a legislative (or Sentencing Commission) decision about which *label* ("sentencing fact" or "element of a greater crime") to affix to one of the facts, namely, the presence of the gun, that will lead to the greater sentence. Given the identity of circumstances apart from the label, the jury's traditional factfinding role, and the law's insistence upon treating like cases alike, why should the legislature's labeling choice make an important *Sixth Amendment* difference?

The Court in *Apprendi,* and now here, concludes that it should not make a difference. The *Sixth Amendment's* jury trial guarantee applies similarly to both. I agree with the majority's analysis, but not with its conclusion. That is to say, I agree that, classically speaking, the difference between a traditional sentencing factor and an element of a greater offense often comes down to a legislative choice about which label to affix. But I cannot jump from there to the conclusion that the *Sixth Amendment* always requires identical treatment of the two scenarios. That jump is fraught with consequences that threaten the fairness of our traditional criminal justice system; it distorts historical sentencing or criminal trial practices; and it upsets settled law on which legislatures have relied in designing punishment systems.

* * *

The majority ignores the adverse consequences inherent in its conclusion. As a result of the majority's rule, sentencing must now take one of three forms, each of which risks either impracticality, unfairness, or harm to the jury trial right the majority purports to strengthen. This circumstance shows that the majority's *Sixth Amendment* interpretation cannot be right.

A

A first option for legislators is to create a simple, pure or nearly pure "charge offense" or "determinate" sentencing system. See Breyer, The Federal Sentencing Guidelines and the Key Compromises upon Which They Rest, *17 Hofstra L. Rev. 1, 8–9 (1988).* In such a system, an indictment would charge a few facts which, taken together, constitute a crime, such as robbery. Robbery would carry a single sentence, say, five years' imprisonment. And every person convicted of robbery would receive that sentence—just as, centuries ago, everyone convicted of almost any serious crime was sentenced to death. See, *e.g.,* Lillquist, The Puzzling Return of Jury Sentencing: Misgivings About *Apprendi*, *82 N. C. L. Rev. 621, 630 (2004).*

Such a system assures uniformity, but at intolerable costs. First, simple determinate sentencing systems impose identical punishments on people who committed their crimes in very different ways. When dramatically different conduct ends up being punished the same way, an injustice has taken place. Simple determinate sentencing has the virtue of treating like cases alike, but it simultaneously fails to treat different cases differently. Some commentators have leveled this charge at sentencing guideline systems themselves. See, *e.g.,* Schulhofer, Assessing the Federal Sentencing Process: The Problem Is Uniformity, Not Disparity, *29 Am. Crim. L. Rev. 833, 847 (1992)* (arguing that the "most important problem under the [Federal] Guidelines system is not too much disparity, but rather excessive uniformity" and arguing for adjustments, including elimination of mandatory minimums, to make the Guidelines system more responsive to relevant differences). The charge is doubly applicable to simple "pure charge" systems that permit no departures from the prescribed sentences, even in extraordinary cases.

Second, in a world of statutorily fixed mandatory sentences for many crimes, determinate sentencing gives tremendous power to prosecutors to manipulate sentences through their choice of charges. Prosecutors can simply charge, or threaten to charge, defendants with crimes bearing higher mandatory sentences. Defendants, knowing that they will not have a chance to argue for a lower sentence in front of a judge, may plead to charges that they might otherwise contest. Considering that most criminal cases do not go to trial and resolution by plea bargaining is the norm, the rule of *Apprendi*, to the extent it results in a return to determinate sentencing, threatens serious unfairness. See Bibas, Judicial Fact–Finding and Sentence Enhancements in a World of Guilty Pleas, *110 Yale L. J. 1097, 1100–1101 (2001)* (explaining that the rule of *Apprendi* hurts defendants by depriving them of sentencing hearings, "the only hearings they were likely to have"; forcing defendants to surrender sentencing issues like drug quantity when they agree to the plea; and transferring power to prosecutors).

B

A second option for legislators is to return to a system of indeterminate sentencing.... Under indeterminate systems, the length of the sentence is entirely or almost entirely within the discretion of the judge or of the parole board, which typically has broad power to decide when to release a prisoner.

When such systems were in vogue, they were criticized, and rightly so, for producing unfair disparities, including race-based disparities, in the punishment of similarly situated defendants. The length of time a person spent in prison appeared to depend on "what the judge ate for breakfast" on the day of sentencing, on which judge you got, or on other factors that should not have made a difference to the length of the sentence.... And under such a system, the judge could vary the sentence greatly based upon his findings about how the defendant had committed the crime—findings that might not have been made by a "preponderance of the evidence," much less "beyond a reasonable doubt." ...

Returning to such a system would ... do little to "ensure [the] control" of what the majority calls "the peopl[e,]" *i.e.*, the jury, "in the judiciary," since "the people" would only decide the defendant's guilt, a finding with no effect on the duration of the sentence. While "the judge's authority to sentence" would formally derive from the jury's verdict, the jury would exercise little or no control over the sentence itself. It is difficult to see how such an outcome protects the structural safeguards the majority claims to be defending.

C

A third option is that which the Court seems to believe legislators will in fact take. That is the option of retaining structured schemes that attempt to punish similar conduct similarly and different conduct differently, but modifying them to conform to *Apprendi*'s dictates. Judges would be able to depart *downward* from presumptive sentences upon finding that mitigating factors were present, but would not be able to depart *upward* unless the prosecutor charged the aggravating fact to a jury and proved it beyond a reasonable doubt. The majority argues, based on the single example of Kansas, that most legislatures will enact amendments along these lines in the face of the oncoming *Apprendi* train. It is therefore worth exploring how this option could work in practice, as well as the assumptions on which it depends.

1

This option can be implemented in one of two ways. The first way would be for legislatures to subdivide each crime into a list of complex crimes, each of which would be defined to include commonly found sentencing factors such as drug quantity, type of victim, presence of violence, degree of injury, use of gun, and so on. A legislature, for example, might enact a robbery statute, modeled on robbery sentencing guidelines, that increases punishment depending upon (1) the nature of the institution robbed, (2) the (a) presence of, (b) brandishing of, (c) other use of, a firearm, (3) making of a death threat, (4) presence of (a) ordinary, (b) serious, (c) permanent or life threatening, bodily injury, (5) abduction, (6) physical restraint, (7) taking of a firearm, (8) taking of drugs, (9) value of property loss, etc. Cf. United States Sentencing Commission, Guidelines Manual § 2B3.1 (Nov. 2003) (hereinafter USSG).

This possibility is, of course, merely a highly calibrated form of the "pure charge" system discussed in Part I–A, *supra*. And it suffers from some of the same defects. The prosecutor, through control of the precise charge, controls the punishment, thereby marching the sentencing system directly away from, not toward, one important guideline goal: rough uniformity of punishment for those who engage in roughly the same *real* criminal conduct. The artificial (and consequently unfair) nature of the resulting sentence is aggravated by the fact that prosecutors must charge all relevant facts about the way the crime was committed before a presentence investigation examines the criminal conduct, perhaps before the trial itself, *i.e.*, before many of the facts relevant to punishment are known.

This "complex charge offense" system also prejudices defendants who seek trial, for it can put them in the untenable position of contesting material aggravating facts in the guilt phases of their trials. Consider a defendant who is charged, not with mere possession of cocaine, but with the specific offense of possession of more than 500 grams of cocaine. Or consider a defendant charged, not with murder, but with the new crime of murder using a machete. Or consider a defendant whom the prosecution wants to claim was a "supervisor," rather than an ordinary gang member. How can a Constitution that guarantees due process put these defendants, as a matter of course, in the position of arguing, "I did not sell drugs, and if I did, I did not sell more than 500 grams" or, "I did not kill him, and if I did, I did not use a machete," or "I did not engage in gang activity, and certainly not as a supervisor" to a single jury? The system can tolerate this kind of problem up to a point (consider the defendant who wants to argue innocence, and, in the alternative, second-degree, not first-degree, murder). But a rereading of the many distinctions made in a typical robbery guideline, suggests that an effort to incorporate any real set of guidelines in a complex statute would reach well beyond that point.

The majority announces that there really is no problem here because "States may continue to offer judicial factfinding as a matter of course to all defendants who plead guilty" and defendants may "stipulate to the relevant facts or consent to judicial factfinding." The problem, of course, concerns defendants who do not want to plead guilty to those elements that, until recently, were commonly thought of as sentencing factors. As to those defendants, the fairness problem arises because States may very well decide that they will *not* permit defendants to carve subsets of facts out of the new, *Apprendi*-required 17–element robbery crime, seeking a judicial determination as to some of those facts and a jury determination as to others. Instead, States may simply require defendants to plead guilty to all 17 elements or proceed with a (likely prejudicial) trial on all 17 elements.

The majority does not deny that States may make this choice; it simply fails to understand *why* any State would want to exercise it. The answer is, as I shall explain in a moment, that the alternative may prove too expensive and unwieldy for States to provide. States that offer defendants the option of judicial factfinding as to some facts (*i.e.,* sentencing facts), say, because of fairness concerns, will also have to offer the defendant a second sentencing jury—just as Kansas has done. I therefore turn to that alternative.

2

The second way to make sentencing guidelines *Apprendi*-compliant would be to require at least two juries for each defendant whenever aggravating facts are present: one jury to determine guilt of the crime charged, and an additional jury to try the disputed facts that, if found, would aggravate the sentence. Our experience with bifurcated trials in the capital punishment context suggests that requiring them for run-of-the-mill sentences would be costly, both in money and in judicial time and resources. Cf. Kozinski & Gallagher, Death: The Ultimate Run–On Sentence, *46 Case W. Res. L. Rev. 1, 13–15*, and n. 64 (1995) (estimating the costs of each capital case at around $1 million more than each noncapital case); Tabak, How Empirical Studies Can Affect Positively the Politics of the Death Penalty, *83 Cornell L. Rev. 1431, 1439–1440 (1998)* (attributing the greater cost of death penalty cases in part to bifurcated proceedings). In the context of noncapital crimes, the potential need for a second indictment alleging aggravating facts, the likely need for formal evidentiary rules to prevent prejudice, and the increased difficulty of obtaining relevant sentencing information, all will mean greater complexity, added cost, and further delay. Indeed, cost and delay could lead legislatures to revert to the complex charge offense system described in Part I–C–1, *supra*.

The majority refers to an *amicus curiae* brief filed by the Kansas Appellate Defender Office, which suggests that a two-jury system has proved workable in Kansas. And that may be so. But in all likelihood, any such workability reflects an uncomfortable fact, a fact at which the majority hints, *ante,* at 14, but whose constitutional implications it does not seem to grasp. The uncomfortable fact that could make the system seem workable—even desirable in the minds of some, including defense attorneys—is called "plea bargaining." See Bibas, *110 Yale L. J., at 1150,* and n. 330 (reporting that in 1996, fewer than 4% of adjudicated state felony defendants have jury trials, 5% have bench trials, and 91% plead guilty). See also *ante,* at 14 (making clear that plea bargaining applies). The Court can announce that the Constitution requires at least two jury trials for each criminal defendant—one for guilt, another for sentencing—but only because it knows full well that more than 90% of defendants will not go to trial even once, much less insist on two or more trials.

What will be the consequences of the Court's holding for the 90% of defendants who do not go to trial? The truthful answer is that we do not know. Some defendants may receive bargaining advantages if the increased cost of the "double jury trial" guarantee makes prosecutors more willing to cede certain sentencing issues to the defense. Other defendants may be hurt if a "single-jury-decides-all" approach makes them more reluctant to risk a trial—perhaps because they want to argue that they did not know what was in the cocaine bag, that it was a small amount regardless, that they were unaware a confederate had a gun, etc. See Bibas, *110 Yale L. J., at 1100* ("Because for many defendants going to trial is not a desirable option, they are left without any real hearings at all"); *id., at 1151* ("The trial right does little good when most defendants do not go to trial").

Increased plea bargaining, less jury trials – majority seeks to protect jury trials

At the least, the greater expense attached to trials and their greater complexity, taken together in the context of an overworked criminal justice system, will likely mean, other things being equal, fewer trials and a greater reliance upon plea bargaining—a system in which punishment is set not by judges or juries but by advocates acting under bargaining constraints. At the same time, the greater power of the prosecutor to control the punishment through the charge would likely weaken the relation between real conduct and real punishment as well. See, *e.g.,* Schulhofer, *29 Am. Crim. L. Rev., at 845* (estimating that evasion of the proper sentence under the Federal Guidelines may now occur in 20%–35% of all guilty plea cases). Even if the Court's holding does not further embed plea-bargaining practices (as I fear it will), its success depends upon the existence of present practice. I do not understand how the *Sixth Amendment* could *require* a sentencing system that will work in practice only if no more than a handful of defendants exercise their right to a jury trial.

The majority's only response is to state that "bargaining over elements . . . probably favors the defendant," adding that many criminal defense lawyers favor its position. But the basic problem is not one of "fairness" to defendants or, for that matter, "fairness" to prosecutors. Rather, it concerns the greater fairness of a sentencing system that a more uniform correspondence between real criminal conduct and real punishment helps to create. At a minimum, a two-jury system, by preventing a judge from taking account of an aggravating fact without the prosecutor's acquiescence, would undercut, if not nullify, legislative efforts to ensure through guidelines that punishments reflect a convicted offender's real criminal conduct, rather than that portion of the offender's conduct that a prosecutor decides to charge and prove.

Efforts to tie real punishment to real conduct are not new. They are embodied in well-established pre-guidelines sentencing practices—practices under which a judge, looking at a presentence report, would seek to tailor the sentence in significant part to fit the criminal conduct in which the offender actually engaged. For more than a century, questions of *punishment* (not those of guilt or innocence) have reflected determinations made, not only by juries, but also by judges, probation officers, and executive parole boards. Such truth-seeking determinations have rested upon both adversarial and non-adversarial processes. The Court's holding undermines efforts to reform these processes, for it means that legislatures cannot *both* permit judges to base sentencing upon real conduct *and* seek, through guidelines, to make the results more uniform.

In these and other ways, the two-jury system would work a radical change in pre-existing criminal law. It is not surprising that this Court has never previously suggested that the Constitution—outside the unique context of the death penalty—might require bifurcated jury-based sentencing. And it is the impediment the Court's holding poses to legislative efforts to achieve that greater systematic fairness that casts doubt on its constitutional validity.

D

Is there a fourth option? Perhaps. Congress and state legislatures might, for example, rewrite their criminal codes, attaching astronomically high sentences to each crime, followed by long lists of mitigating facts, which, for the most part, would consist of the absence of aggravating facts.... But political impediments to legislative action make such rewrites difficult to achieve; and it is difficult to see why the *Sixth Amendment* would require legislatures to undertake them.

It may also prove possible to find combinations of, or variations upon, my first three options. But I am unaware of any variation that does not involve (a) the shift of power to the prosecutor (weakening the connection between real conduct and real punishment) inherent in any charge offense system, (b) the lack of uniformity inherent in any system of pure judicial discretion, or (c) the complexity, expense, and increased reliance on plea bargains involved in a "two-jury" system. The simple fact is that the design of any fair sentencing system must involve efforts to make practical compromises among competing goals. The majority's reading of the *Sixth Amendment* makes the effort to find those compromises—already difficult—virtually impossible.

II

* * *

Given history's silence on the question of laws that structure a judge's discretion within the range provided by the legislatively labeled maximum term, it is not surprising that our modern, pre-*Apprendi* cases made clear that legislatures could, within broad limits, distinguish between "sentencing facts'' and ''elements of crimes.'' See *McMillan, 477 U.S., at 85–88, 91 L. Ed. 2d 67, 106 S. Ct. 2411*. By their choice of label, legislatures could indicate whether a judge or a jury must make the relevant factual determination. History does not preclude legislatures from making this decision. And, as I argued in Part I, *supra,* allowing legislatures to structure sentencing in this way has the dual effect of enhancing and giving meaning to the *Sixth Amendment's* jury trial right as to core crimes, while affording additional due process to defendants in the form of sentencing hearings before judges—hearings the majority's rule will eliminate for many.

Is there a risk of unfairness involved in permitting Congress to make this labeling decision? Of course. As we have recognized, the ''tail'' of the sentencing fact might ''wag the dog of the substantive offense.'' *McMillan, supra, at 88, 91 L. Ed. 2d 67, 106 S. Ct. 2411*. Congress might permit a judge to sentence an individual for murder though convicted only of making an illegal lane change. See *ante,* at 10 (majority opinion). But that is the kind of problem that the *Due Process Clause* is well suited to cure. *McMillan* foresaw the possibility that judges would have to use their own judgment in dealing with such a problem; but that is what judges are there for. And, as Part I, *supra,* makes clear, the alternatives are worse—not only practically, but, although the majority refuses to admit it, constitutionally as well.

Historic practice . . . does not compel the result the majority reaches. And constitutional concerns counsel the opposite.

III

The majority also overlooks important institutional considerations. Congress and the States relied upon what they believed was their constitutional power to decide, within broad limits, whether to make a particular fact (a) a sentencing factor or (b) an element in a greater crime. They relied upon *McMillan* as guaranteeing the constitutional validity of that proposition. They created sentencing reform, an effort to change the criminal justice system so that it reflects systematically not simply upon guilt or innocence but also upon what should be done about this now-guilty offender. Those efforts have spanned a generation. They have led to state sentencing guidelines and the Federal Sentencing Guideline system. . . . These systems are imperfect and they yield far from perfect results, but I cannot believe the Constitution forbids the state legislatures and Congress to adopt such systems and to try to improve them over time. Nor can I believe that the Constitution hamstrings legislatures in the way that JUSTICE O'CONNOR and I have discussed.

IV

Now, let us return to the question I posed at the outset. Why does the *Sixth Amendment* permit a jury trial right (in respect to a particular fact) to depend upon a legislative labeling decision, namely, the legislative decision to label the fact a *sentencing fact*, instead of an *element of the crime?* The answer is that the fairness and effectiveness of a sentencing system, and the related fairness and effectiveness of the criminal justice system itself, depends upon the legislature's possessing the constitutional authority (within due process limits) to make that labeling decision. To restrict radically the legislature's power in this respect, as the majority interprets the *Sixth Amendment* to do, prevents the legislature from seeking sentencing systems that are consistent with, and indeed may help to advance, the Constitution's greater fairness goals.

To say this is not simply to express concerns about fairness to defendants. It is also to express concerns about the serious practical (or impractical) changes that the Court's decision seems likely to impose upon the criminal process; about the tendency of the Court's decision to embed further plea bargaining processes that lack transparency and too often mean nonuniform, sometimes arbitrary, sentencing practices; about the obstacles the Court's decision poses to legislative efforts to bring about greater uniformity between real criminal conduct and real punishment; and ultimately about the limitations that the Court imposes upon legislatures' ability to make democratic legislative decisions. Whatever the faults of guidelines systems—and there are many—they are more likely to find their cure in legislation emerging from the experience of, and discussion among, all elements of the criminal justice community, than in a virtually unchangeable constitutional decision of this Court.

V

Taken together these three sets of considerations, concerning consequences, concerning history, concerning institutional reliance, leave me where I was in *Apprendi, i.e.,* convinced that the Court is wrong. Until now, I would have thought the Court might have limited *Apprendi* so that its underlying principle would not undo sentencing reform efforts. Today's case dispels that illusion. At a minimum, the case sets aside numerous state efforts in that direction. Perhaps the Court will distinguish the Federal Sentencing Guidelines, but I am uncertain how. As a result of today's decision, federal prosecutors, like state prosecutors, must decide what to do next, how to handle tomorrow's case.

Consider some of the matters that federal prosecutors must know about, or guess about, when they prosecute their next case: (1) Does today's decision apply in full force to the Federal Sentencing Guidelines? (2) If so, must the initial indictment contain all sentencing factors, charged as "elements" of the crime? (3) What, then, are the evidentiary rules? Can the prosecution continue to use, say presentence reports, with their conclusions reflecting layers of hearsay? Cf. *Crawford v. Washington, 541 U.S. ___, ___, ___–___, 158 L. Ed. 2d 177, 124 S. Ct. 1354 (2004) (slip op., at 27, 32–33)* (clarifying the *Sixth Amendment's* requirement of confrontation with respect to testimonial hearsay). Are the numerous cases of this Court holding that a sentencing judge may consider virtually any reliable information still good law when juries, not judges, are required to determine the matter? See, *e.g., United States v. Watts, 519 U.S. 148, 153–157, 136 L. Ed. 2d 554, 117 S. Ct. 633 (1997) (per curiam)* (evidence of conduct of which the defendant has been acquitted may be considered at sentencing). Cf. *Witte v. United States, 515 U.S. 389, 399–401, 132 L. Ed. 2d 351, 115 S. Ct. 2199 (1995)* (evidence of uncharged criminal conduct used in determining sentence). (4) How are juries to deal with highly complex or open-ended

Sentencing Guidelines obviously written for application by an experienced trial judge? See, *e.g.*, USSG § 3B1.1 (requiring a greater sentence when the defendant was a leader of a criminal activity that involved four or more participants or was "*otherwise extensive*" (emphasis added)); § § 3D1.1–3D1.2 (highly complex "multiple count" rules); § 1B1.3 (relevant conduct rules).

Ordinarily, this Court simply waits for cases to arise in which it can answer such questions. But this case affects tens of thousands of criminal prosecutions, including federal prosecutions. Federal prosecutors will proceed with those prosecutions subject to the risk that all defendants in those cases will have to be sentenced, perhaps tried, anew. Given this consequence and the need for certainty, I would not proceed further piecemeal; rather, I would call for further argument on the ramifications of the concerns I have raised. But that is not the Court's view.

For the reasons given, I dissent.

CHAPTER 23

Appellate and Other Post–Trial Remedies Federal Habeas Corpus

D. Federal Prisoners

Add as section D to page 1679:

In *Hamdi v. Rumsfeld*, ___ U.S. ___, 124 S.Ct. 2633 (2004) the Court upheld the right of the federal government to detain enemy combatants. However, the Court held that such a detainee would retain the right of habeas corpuse 28 U.S.C. § 2241.

The statute governing habeas corpus allowed aliens detained in Guantanamo Bay Naval Base in Cuba, a territory over which the United States government exercised plenary and exclusive jurisdiction to pursue petitions for writs of habeas corpus. The statute conferred jurisdiction over these cases in United States courts. *Rasul v. Bush*, ___ U.S. ___, 124 S.Ct. 2686 (2004).

†